SUMMER SAIL II

Visiting Northern Lake Michigan

by

John B. Torinus

LARANMARK PRESS
A division of Laranmark, Inc   *Neshkoro, Wisconsin*

LARANMARK PRESS

A division of
Laranmark, Inc.
216 Main Street
Box 253
Neshkoro, WI 54960

Copyright © 1985 by John B. Torinus, Sr.
ISBN:
   Leatherbound Limited Edition: 0-910937-54-0
   Hardcover Edition: 0-910937-53-2
   Paperback Edition: 0-910937-52-4

All rights reserved, which include the right
to reproduce this book or any portion thereof in
any form whatsover. For information, address
inquiries to:
Laranmark, Inc.
Box 253
Neshkoro, WI 54960

First Printing June 1985

Cover Art by Keith Ward, Milwaukee

TABLE OF CONTENTS

Introduction 9

Chapter 1
A BRIEF HISTORY......................... 15

Chapter 2
MICHIGAN UNDER THE SEA 23

Chapter 3
CRUISING STARTS AT LELAND 33

Chapter 4
GRAND TRAVERSE BAY 43

Chapter 5
CHARLEVOIX THE BEAUTIFUL........... 55

Chapter 6
LITTLE TRAVERSE BAY 69

Chapter 7
THE STORY OF KING STRANG 79

Chapter 8
THE BEAVER ISLAND GROUP............. 91

Chapter 9
THE ISLAND............................ 101

Chapter 10
  CRUISING WEST TO MANISTIQUE **115**

Chapter 11
  LES CHENEAUX ISLANDS **121**

Chapter 12
  SUGGESTED TWO WEEK CRUISE......... **127**

Appendix................................... **133**

Credits...................................... **143**

Bibliography **145**

Index.. **147**

ACKNOWLEDGEMENTS

The material making up this book falls into three main categories: historical, nautical, and pictorial.

The books and publications from which I obtained the historical material are listed in the bibliography, and visitors to this area might well obtain and peruse some of these to add to the enjoyment of their visit.

The data on harbors and other navigational notes came from two main sources: the Great Lakes Cruising Club's *Port Pilot and Log Book* and the *Michigan Harbors Guide* published by the Michigan Waterways Commission.

The Michigan Travel Bureau provided invaluable help in furnishing many beautiful pictures. The Waterways Commission provided some of the aerial photos of marinas as did photographer Robert T. McCoy of Wauwatosa, Wisconsin.

And once again my sailing friend Rockne Fitzgerald dug into his files for the color picture on the back cover and a number of other black-and-whites.

Major credit for my inspiration to write this book goes to the people who bought my first effort at writing about sailing, Summer Sail I. The nice things they had to say encouraged me to try the same format in another beautiful cruising area. To all of them I dedicate this volume.

SUMMER SAIL II
Visiting
Northern Lake Michigan
by
John B. Torinus

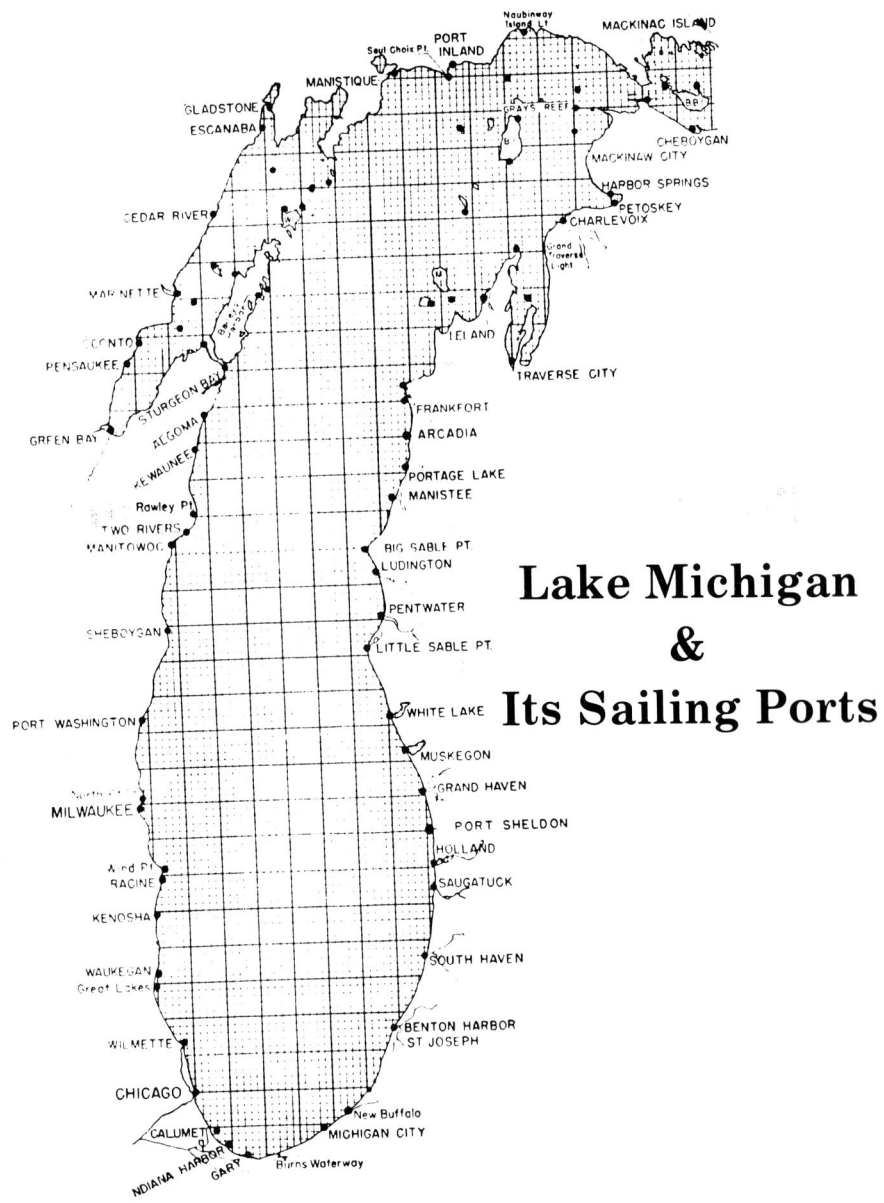

INTRODUCTION

For almost 250 years the only access to the harbors of Lake Michigan was by water; first the canoes of the Indians and the French *voyageurs*, then sailboats and steam-powered craft. The fur trade first attracted white men to this virgin paradise and then came lumbering. But the first hints of the vacation tourist trade were evident as early as the 1860s when steamers brought visitors to harbors like Traverse City and Petoskey and on north to Mackinac Island.

The railroads were pushed northward into the area in the 1870s, and the seeds were sewn for the establishment of colonies of summer residents along the entire northwest shore of Michigan. The building of highways where Indian trails had once been laid put the icing on the cake.

And though most visitors today come by auto, the pristine waters of Lake Michigan are still the finest way to enjoy this vacation wonderland.

The State of Michigan many years ago realized the great potential value of the many miles of shoreline of Lakes Michigan and Huron as well as exposure to Lake Superior in the Upper Peninsula. In 1947 the Michigan Waterways Commission was established with the mission of providing the very finest in harbor facilities along these shorelines for the use of recreational boaters. And in the almost 40 years of its existence the Waterways Commission has developed a string of 66 protected harbors and public marinas. The goal was to locate them in such a way that no boat was ever more than 15 miles from safety, and that goal today is near achievement.

Development of the facilities was a three-way program financed with federal, state, and local money, but the impetus came from the State of Michigan which decided to allocate a percentage of the taxes it collected on the sale of motor fuel to the harbor program. It was estimated that 1.023 percent of the gasoline consumed in Michigan is used by boaters, so this amount of tax revenue was returned to the Waterways Commission for boating purposes.

Once the facilities were developed it became the responsibility of the local municipalities to operate and maintain the marinas. They are allowed to charge fees for the use of the facilities to help with the operation and maintenance costs, but the fees are regulated by the Waterways Commission.

The Waterways Commission also insists that a minimum of 50 percent of the docking space in any given harbor shall be available to transient boaters. In addition where seasonal rentals are accepted, communities reserve the right to rent those wells for transient use when the seasonal renter is on cruise.

Slips are available on a first-come-first-serve basis. It has proven unworkable to accept reservations, but almost all of the marinas are equipped with marine radios and monitor channel 16, and the dockmasters are responsive to calls from boaters approaching the harbor. If all slips are occupied, they normally will arrange for rafting.

Some of the harbors, Leland and Greilickville for example, are designated as harbors of refuge, and those so designated are forbidden to turn away any boat.

Channel 9 is the working channel for most of the marine radios operated by the dockmasters, and boaters are well advised to have this channel available as well as channel 22 which is the Coast Guard working channel.

NOAH radio in this area is based in Traverse City and broadcasts on Weather Channel 2. A word of caution at this point: Weather forecasts are given for both near shore (up to 5 miles from shore) and offshore, and a considerable difference in conditions may be encountered out in Lake Michigan from that along shore. One such condition is pea soup fog, and seldom is there any warning of this in marine broadcasts. Any boaters venturing out on the big lake should be prepared for this eventuality.

One cruising friend prefers to do some of his own weather forecasting and finds the weather map in the daily Detroit *Free Press* a valuable tool in interpreting the upcoming weather.

Following are the chart numbers for various segments of this area:

    14902 — Manitou channel to the Straits of Mackinac
    14912 — Leland and the Manitou Islands
    14913 — Grand Traverse and Little Traverse Bays
    14911 — Beaver Island Group
    14880 — Mackinac Island and east
    14908 — Area west to Manistique

The Waterways Commission in 1983 published a booklet entitled *Michigan Harbors Guide* which lists the facilities available at each of the public marinas along with aerial photographs of the docks. It can be obtained by writing to: P.O. Box 30028, Lansing, MI 48909.

The Great Lakes Cruising Club's *Port Pilot and Log Book* also contains extensive documentation on this area. I have made good use of both in compliling this book. In addition, I explored bookstores, museums, and Chambers of Commerce offices in each of the harbor areas to acquire historical and other background information. The Michigan State Travel Bureau was also most helpful. I have listed this material in the bibiography attached with the thought that reading local history will add much to the pleasure of the yachtsman's visit.

Mackinac Island Today   *Michigan Travel Bureau photo*

Fort Mackinac *Michigan Travel Bureau photo*

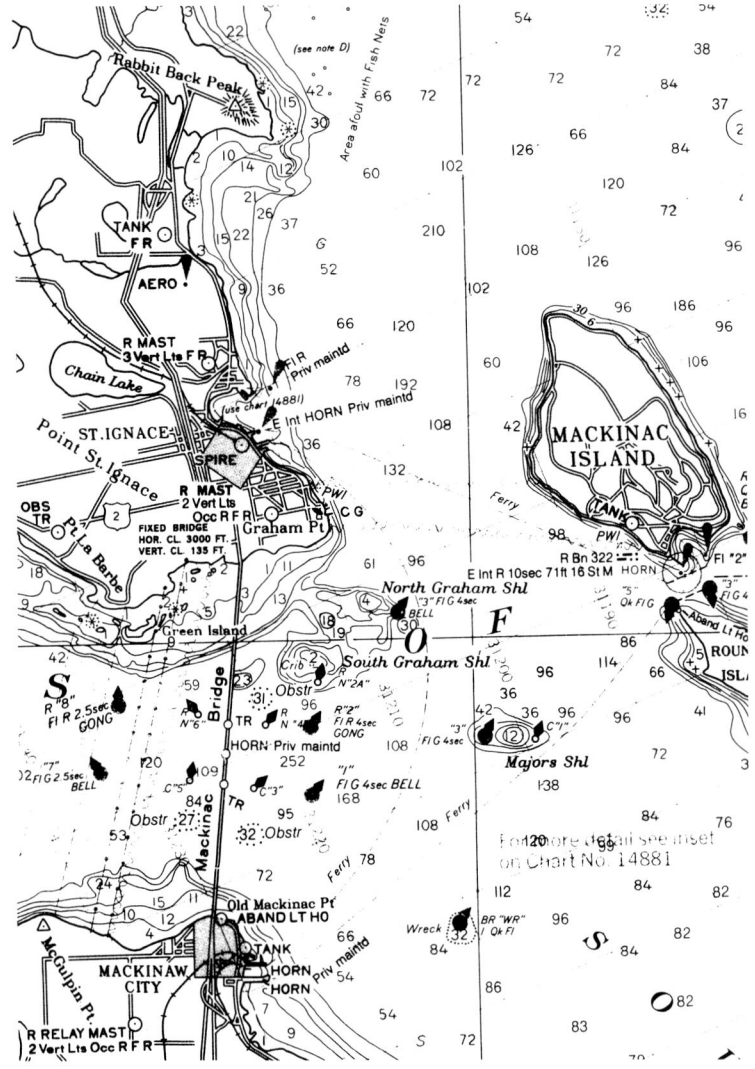

1
A BRIEF HISTORY

There are five choke points around the world where the parade of history has been funneled through narrow passages, the control of which was bitterly contested over the centuries by the major maritime powers. Great Britain controlled four of the five at one time or another: the English Channel; the Straits of Gibraltar; the Suez Canal; and the one with which this book treats, the Straits of Mackinac. The fifth, the Panama Canal, assumed its importance at a later time in history.

The Straits of Mackinac and the island which sits astride them dominated the history of the Northwest Territories of the United States and Canada for the better part of three centuries and were controlled successively by France, England, and the United States. Even Spain at one time took a stab at gaining control over the waterway.

The Ojibway Indians called the island "Michinnimakinong" which translated as follows: MICH — great,

INNI — connecting sound, MAKI — fault, NONG — land or place; literally, the "Land of the Great Fault." The Island has a large crevice or crack, and the term was used by the Indians as an identifying description. The Indian name became "Michilimackinac" in French usage, which was then shortened to "Mackinac."

The British heard the original Indian ending as "aw" and spelled it that way. As a result, all names ending with "ac" are in the Upper Peninsula and all those ending with "aw" are in the Lower Peninsula. Thus, it is Mackinac Island and Mackinac County but Mackinaw City and Mackinaw blankets. But regardless, all are pronounced "aw" and woe be it to the tourist who calls it "ac".

Jean Nicolet is generally credited with being the first white man to visit the Straits. That was in 1634 on his historic mission to find the fabled Northwest Passage to the Orient, the legendary water route that would allow Europeans to reach the Far East by sailing around or through North America. Nicolet wound up at the mouth of the Fox River in Green Bay. His report on the fabulous country he had discovered triggered further exploration and exploitation. Father Jacques Marquette extended Nicolet's voyage until he discovered the Mississippi River. He returned by way of Lake Michigan where he died from exhaustion at a point on the shore near present-day Ludington. He was buried at the mission he had founded at St. Ignace, but the report which his partner Louis Jolliet took back to Montreal further depicted the great natural wealth of the area, particularly the tremendous potential of trading with the Indians for fur pelts.

French *voyageurs* seized the opportunity of acquiring the pelts for beads and baubles and capitalized on the Indians' weakness for alcoholic beverages like brandy.

The fur trade was carried on almost exclusively in birch bark canoes which were patterned after the original designs of the Ojibway Indians. Usually about 40 feet long and four feet wide in the middle, the canoes were made of strips of ¼-inch birch bark sewn together with spruce roots. They were strengthened with a framework of cedar ribs and cross pieces and made water tight by pressing hot pitch into the seams. Their picturesque appearance was heightened by showy designs painted on the gondola-shaped ends. Despite their strength they were easily punctured, so a supply of roots, bark, and pitch was always carried to repair frequent leaks caused by striking snags and stones.

Besides their crew of eight husky men, these fragile and tipsy vessels could carry about four tons of goods and supplies, all of which had to be carefully balanced, and yet they would glide over the water with the buoyancy and stillness of a duck.

The *voyageurs* or canoemen who handled these craft were a singular class of men who survived only as long as the industry which gave them employment. Mostly French *Canadiens*, they were light-hearted half-wild bands of men with flashing eyes and swarthy faces. No Englishman could match them in meeting the privation of the wilderness trade, so they held a virtual monopoly on this calling.

During the spring and summer, these reckless fellows swarmed about Michilimackinac in large numbers. Like a crew of sailors paid off after a long voyage, they devoted themselves to sprees of high living, and in a few weeks of feasting, drinking, dancing, fiddling, and gambling, they would squander their earnings of the winter and then embark upon another expedition into the wilds.

This paragraph from a fascinating book on the history

of Mackinac describes the height of the fur trade in the area:

"It was no unusual thing to see a hundred or more canoes of Indians at once approaching the Island, laden with their articles of traffic, and to these we add the squadrons of large Mackinaw boats constantly arriving from the outposts with the furs, pelts, and buffalo robes collected by the distant traders; some idea may be formed on the extensive operations and important position of the American Fur Company, as well as the vast circle of human beings either immediately or remotely connected with it."

The book from which I quote is *Three Flags at the Straits* by Walter Havighurst, published by Prentice Hall. I highly recommend it as a colorful history of the area.

The French built a fort at St. Ignace in 1694 to protect their interest in the fur trade, and they moved it to the south side of the Straits in 1713 to what is now Mackinaw City. When the British drove the French out of this part of the country the Union Jack was run up the flagpole at the fort, but the British occupation was rather brief. An Indian leader named Pontiac organized all the tribes in the area and attacked the British forts on the lakes, including Mackinaw, where they got inside the stockade on a ruse and perpetrated a horrible massacre of British troops and traders. The British reestablished control a year later and moved the fort to the island in the belief that it was less vulnerable to attack there.

The United States was granted control of this area in the treaty ending the Revolutionary War in 1783, but it wasn't until 1796 that U.S. troops arrived to occupy Fort Mackinaw. Even then the British were not through, and when they declared war again in 1812, a force of British troops sent from Montreal took the island by surprise, forced the U.S. garrison to surrender and again hoisted the Union Jack up the flagpole. The United States sent an expedition to retake the fort in 1814. But the British had been right about locating the fort on the island, and the fort's cannons repelled the waterborne attackers. It was of no great consequence, however, as the peace treaty of 1815 again awarded control of the area to the United States.

American jurisdiction over the entire area was solidified in 1836 in a treaty signed with the Indian tribes of the territory in which over 20 million acres of land were ceded to the government in return for an annual payment to be made to the Indians at a council meeting at Mackinac.

The territories west of the Straits became known as the richest fur domain in the world, and there was a ready market for the various pelts in the East and more particularly in Europe. The Northwest Company was organized to exploit the fur trade in 1784, and then John Jacob Astor arrived on the scene with the American Fur Company in 1808. Astor persuaded the United States Congress to enact a law in 1816 restricting the issuance of licenses to trade for furs with the Indians to American citizens, and he soon had a monopoly on the trade which dominated the commerce of the area through the early part of the 19th century.

In 1819, the first steamboat visited the Straits, a vessel the Indians called "Walk-in-the-Water." Trading posts set up in the interior led to the establishment of settlements like Green Bay, Grand Haven, and finally Chicago which was incorporated as a village in 1833. The opening of the Illinois River Canal, providing water traffic to the Mississippi from Lake Michigan, established Chicago as a metropolis of the Lakes.

What once had been the fabulous fur trade began to taper off in the 1840s, the trappers having killed off the bounty of the woods and streams of the area. And as it did so, the Mackinac economy also declined, and fishing once again became the prime occupation of the settlers who remained.

During the Civil War, the military units were withdrawn from the fort for duty elsewhere, and the Island lived a quiet and peaceful life in contrast to its earlier history.

It was this peace and quiet and the natural beauty of the environment which led to its discovery as a vacation paradise. In the 1870s, steamers began to transport visitors to the Island from nearby ports such as Petoskey and Traverse City and more distant population centers such as Detroit and Chicago. Congress established the Island as a national park in 1875, the second only to Yellowstone in the National Park System. In the 1880s, the government began selling lots to private individuals for the building of summer residences there. A number of hotels were erected, and the old Mission House was converted into a tourist facility. In 1887 the elegant Grand Hotel opened its doors to guests; its beautiful portico veranda looking out over the harbor.

The final troop evacuation came in 1894, and in 1895 the U.S. government transferred title to the Island to the State of Michigan for a state park.

The tourist industry almost totally dominated Mackinac's history in the 20th century, climaxed by the building of the bridge across the Straits, a project which took three years before its opening in 1957.

Under this bridge today sail some of the finest yachts of the Great Lakes, particularly at the conclusion of the annual Chicago to Mackinac Race in which a total of 300 boats compete by invitation in this 333-mile event. And when the crews gather in the harbor at race's end it reminds one of the days a century or more before when the *voyageurs* arrived in late spring with their harvest of furs. The socializing is the same, even if a bit more sophisticated, and once again the Island becomes a rendezvous for men — and today women — of the lakes.

The Straits are the starting point — the choke point, if you will — for fascinating cruises in all directions: to the east into Lake Huron, the North Channel, and Georgian Bay; to the south into Lake Huron and Saginaw Bay; to the northwest up the St. Mary's River into Lake Superior; to the west and south into Lake Michigan and Green Bay.

In *Summer Sail: Cruising Green Bay's Historic Waters*, I took you cruising into Green Bay. This volume will cover the enchanting waters and harbors of northern Lake Michigan.

Fort Mackinac Today   *Michigan Travel Bureau photo*

2

MICHIGAN UNDER THE SEA

In my book *Summer Sail: Cruising Green Bay's Historic Waters*, I remarked that if you and your boat had been around these parts 350 million years ago you would have enjoyed sailing on a large tropical sea which covered most of the Great Lakes basin and all of the Lower Pensinsula of the present state of Michigan. This was the Silurian Sea, a prime feature of the geological history of this area during the Devonian Period of the earth's formation. Popularly called the "Age of Fishes," the Devonian Period lasted about 50 million years. It derived its name from the English county of Devon where formations of this period were first studied about 1840.

At the beginning of the Devonian Period, North America had much the same shape as it has today except that an arm of the Atlantic Ocean covered much of the

GEOLOGICAL TIME SCALE

Read from bottom to top.

ERAS	TIME PERIODS ROCK SYSTEMS	TIME EPOCHS ROCK SERIES	APPROX. DURATION MILLION YEARS	APPROX. PERCENT TOTAL AGE	LIFE FORMS
CENOZOIC	QUATERNARY	RECENT PLEISTOCENE	1	2	Rise and dominance of Man.
CENOZOIC	UPPER TERTIARY	PLIOCENE MIOCENE	65	2	Modern animals and plants.
CENOZOIC	LOWER TERTIARY	OLIGOCENE EOCENE PALEOCENE	65	2	Rapid development of modern mammals, insects, and plants.
MESOZOIC	UPPER CRETACEOUS		75	5	Primitive mammals; last dinosaurs; last ammonites.
MESOZOIC	LOWER CRETACEOUS		75	5	Rise of flowering plants.
MESOZOIC	JURASSIC		45	5	First birds, first mammals. Diversification of reptiles; climax of ammonites; coniferous trees.
MESOZOIC	TRIASSIC		45	5	Rise of dinosaurs; cycadlike plants; bony fishes.
PALEOZOIC	PERMIAN		45	9	Rise of reptiles. Modern insects. Last of many plant and animal groups.
PALEOZOIC	PENNSYLVANIAN } CARBONIFEROUS		75	9	First reptiles. Amphibians; primitive insects; seed ferns; primitive conifers.
PALEOZOIC	MISSISSIPPIAN } CARBONIFEROUS		75	9	Climax of shell-crushing sharks. Primitive ammonites.
PALEOZOIC	DEVONIAN		50	9	First amphibians, first land snails. Primitive land plants. Climax of brachiopods.
PALEOZOIC	SILURIAN		20	9	First traces of land life. Scorpions. First lungfishes. Widespread coral reefs.
PALEOZOIC	ORDOVICIAN		70	9	First fish. Climax of trilobites. First appearance of many marine invertebrates.
PALEOZOIC	CAMBRIAN		50	9	First marine invertebrates, including trilobites.
	PROTEROZOIC } PRE-CAMBRIAN		About 3000	84	First signs of life. Algae.
	ARCHEOZOIC } PRE-CAMBRIAN		About 3000	84	

Age of oldest dated rocks: about 3,500,000,000 years.

east coast and extended inland as far west as present-day Oklahoma, leaving a large sub-continent on the high ground known as Appalachia. In the middle of the period this warm Devonian sea spread northward covering most of the Middle West.

The chief life forms of the period were marine invertebrates, including coral echinoderms, trilobites, and brachiopods. Fossils of all of these forms of early life are now found in various places in the Great Lakes region.

One of these fossils is known today as the Petoskey stone, the state stone of Michigan. Prized among beachcombers these beautiful oval stones are found along the sand beaches of the eastern shore of Lake Michigan and are particularly common in the Petoskey area. Hence the name.

The Petoskey stone was once a living section of a colony of coral which formed giant reefs along the whole western border of what is now the Lower Peninsula of the state of Michigan as well as the eastern shore of Lake Huron. (See chart.)

Over a period of millions of years silt, black mud, and other sediments fell to the bottom of the Silurian Sea, covering the remains of the dead coral and eventually filling in the Michigan basin as the warm sea retreated. Heat and pressure transformed the coral and sediment into rock. Relieved of the pressure of the sea the state of Michigan gradually rose, forming the relatively flat surface which we know as the Lower Peninsula.

The other major event which shaped the present land and water surface of the area was the coming of the giant glaciers during the Ice Age, a rather recent event in terms of geological history. The glaciers bulldozed giant trenches in the land surface in some areas, in others dumping heaps of debris as they advanced and then

PETOSKEY STONE - A PETRIFIED CORAL FOSSIL

MICHIGAN'S OFFICIAL STATE STONE

The PETOSKEY STONE is composed of the fossilized skeletons of "Colony Coral" (Hexagonaria Pericarnata; Sloss) which lived their life span in the warm waters that covered Michigan during the Devonian Period some 350 million years ago. Each hexagonal chamber contains the prehistoric remains of a salt water marine life.

What is often referred to as the "eye" of the hexagonal chamber is, in reality, the mouth of the coral. The radiating lines from the mouth were the tentacles which drew microscopic food to the coral's mouth.

Flecks in the mouth or on the tentacles of the coral is this prehistoric food which has petrified with the coral through the millions of years.

Dark streaks sometimes found in the stone is the silt which buried the coral when Michigan's warm, salt water sea retreated and mostly serves to enhance the natural beauty and history of the stone.

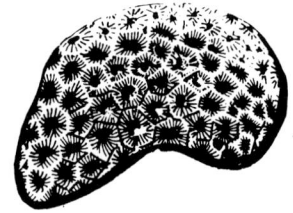  

Copyright 1975

retreated. The melt from the glacier eventually filled the Michigan basin, forming Lakes Michigan and Huron.

The glaciers also scraped away layers of silt and sediment in some areas, exposing the fossilized coral which have become known as Petoskey stones. They are the fossils of the Hexagonaria Coral, aptly named for the hexagonial chambers of each once-living coral. If the eye of each chamber is examined closely, there are rays extending outward from this eye. The eye was the mouth of the coral, and the radiating lines were the tentacles which drew microscopic food to the coral's mouth. Flecks in the mouth or the tentacles is that prehistoric food which was petrified through millions of years. Dark streaks sometimes found in the stone are the remains of the silt which buried the coral, serving to enhance its natural beauty.

The Petoskey stone is easily identified. When dry it is whitish-gray, oval in shape, and powdery to the touch. When wet, the hexagonial pattern of the fossil is clearly visible. It can be almost any size or weight. Good stones are judged on the clarity and consistency of the eyes and rays. They are easily polished and made into beautiful jewelry.

If you wish to acquire some Petoskey stone on your visit to this area and do not have the time or inclination to search for them along the beaches, they are readily available along with fine jewelry made from the stone in gift stores in any of the resort communities.

Two other geological features of the landscape deserve mention. At one time there was a tilted layer of limestone which formed a high ridge running north and south, off the western shore of Lake Michigan. The glaciers buried the ridge under a blanket of debris, but some bluffs remain, making up the string of islands which start with South

Manitou and proceed north all the way to the Straits of Mackinac.

The other feature is the formation of the spectacular sand dunes along much of the eastern shore of the lake. The major influence in the creation of this formation was the prevailing southwest winds. The building of the dunes is a dynamic and everchanging process. The winds blow sand from the dry part of the beach inland until it is deposited behind some obstacle. Once a sandpile accumulates it then provides a wind shadow which causes sand to be deposited on its lee side. As this process continues, sand erodes from the windward side of the dune, then moves up its face to accumulate just over the edge on the lee side. As it builds up it periodically avalanches down this steep face, and by this process the dune migrates inland while a new dune develops on the beach. The younger dunes decrease the sand supply from the beach and block the wind so that vegetation becomes established on the older dune and it is stabilized.

Thus, the shore of Lake Michigan is a dynamic shifting boundary between land and water and has been so since its earliest ancestor. One would think that prudent individuals would stay clear of this fragile lake margin in choosing construction sites. But development along Lake Michigan belies this concern and shows a complete lack of respect for geologic processes.

Fortunately, more and more of these unstable bluffs are being placed under restrictive zoning and a buffer of lakeside parks is being established along the shoreline. One such park is Sleeping Bear Dunes National Lakeshore Park extending from Point Betsie on the south to Leland on the north, including North and South Manitou Islands.

Indian legend has it that a mother bear and her two cubs

fled a forest fire in Wisconsin by swimming across Lake Michigan. The mother bear reached the Michigan shore and climbed a steep bluff to await her cubs. The cubs, exhausted by the long swim, never reached land. The mother bear waited day after day to no avail. Finally, she died. The Great Spirit Manitou marked the mother's resting place with a mound of sand now called Sleeping Bear Dune and then created the Manitou Islands in the lake where the two cubs drowned.

The dunes of Sleeping Bear Park provide a spectacular scene for the yachtsman approaching the Leelanau Peninsula.

And it is here that we begin our summer sail into this beautiful area.

Sleeping Bear Dunes *Michigan Travel Bureau photo*

Dunes Line Michigan Shore   *Michigan Travel Bureau photo*

Beachcombing For Petoskey Stones
Michigan Travel Bureau photo

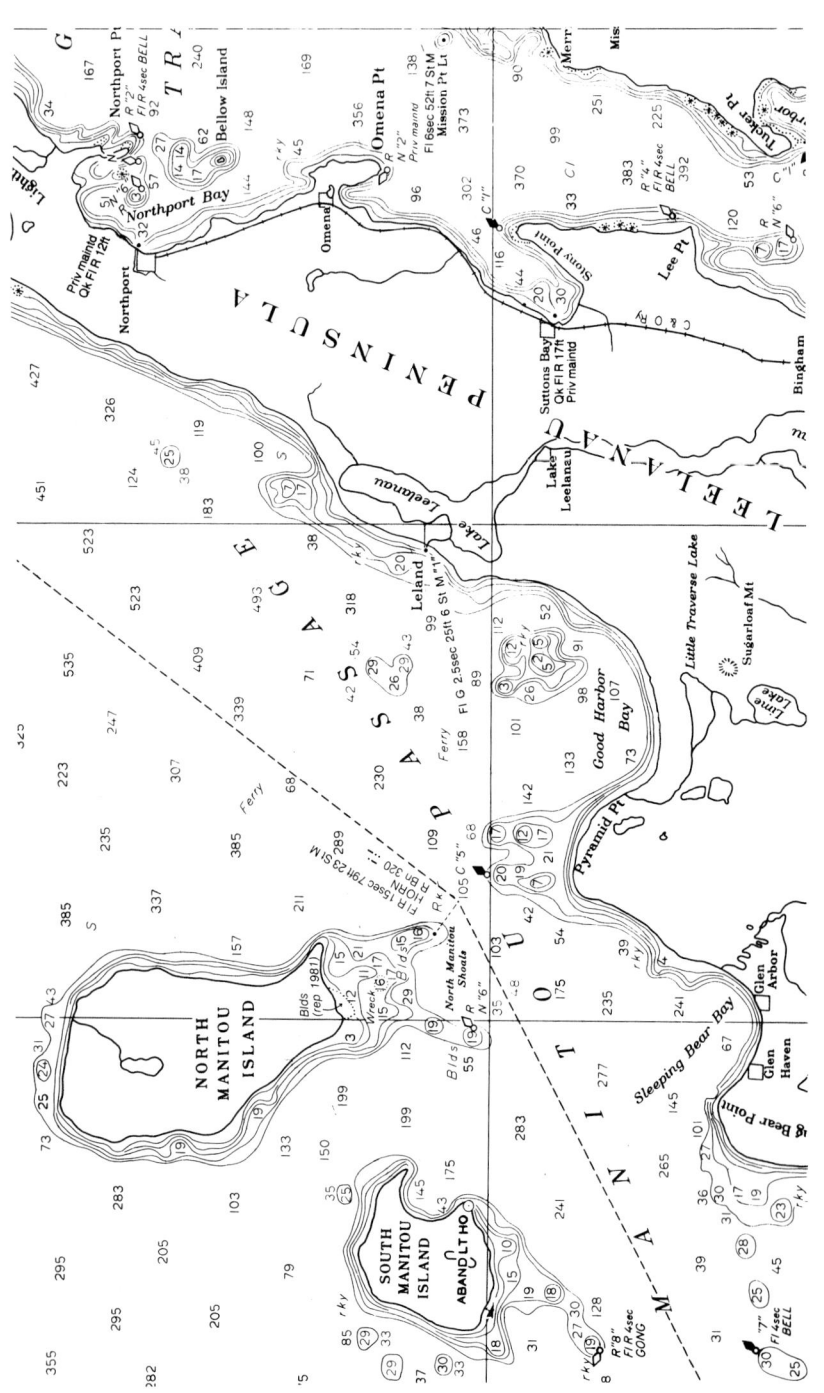

3

CRUISING STARTS AT LELAND

Looking at a map large enough to show both sides of Lake Michigan, Navigation Chart 14902 as an example, there is a striking resemblance between the general geography of both sides of the lake in the vicinity of the 45th parallel.

Grand Traverse Bay on the east side is somewhat comparable with the Bay of Green Bay on the west shore, and the so-called Little Finger of Michigan, the Leelanau Peninsula, is the counterpart of Door County in Wisconsin. The Leland area is the beginning of the fine cruising water on the east shore of Lake Michigan, extending north to the Straits of Mackinac.

The origin of the name Leelanau is shrouded in mystery. The original assumption was that it was an Indian name given the area by the tribes who roamed this

Leland   Robert T. McCoy photo

Fish Town At Leland *Michigan Travel Bureau photo*

heavily wooded shore making trails which are today's highways, marking them with bent-over saplings and giving Indian names to various locations. But they left no records, only legends. We do know that there was a village of some 300 Ottawa Indians on a hill north of present-day Leland which the Indians called "Mishi-mi-go-bing," meaning "the place where the Indian canoe ran up the river because there was no harbor." It was this river which attracted the settlement which became today's Leland.

Surprisingly, there are no written records of this area until 1836, although we know that French explorers moved through these waters in the mid-17th century. It is now believed that the name Leelanau is of French origin, based on the fact that the area is on the lee side of the lake and that the "eau" or "au" is more likely the French spelling for water.

The first white settlers were attracted by the dense hardwood forests, a thriving business in those days being the furnishing of hardwood logs to the steamers which plied the waters of the lake and used wood in their boilers. The hardwood logs were cut to four-foot lengths and split. The business was known as "wooding," and it was in 1840 that a wooding station was established here.

As coal gradually replaced wood as the fuel for the steam boilers, the lumbermen turned to milling the products of the forests into lumber. The waterpower of the river was first harnessed by the building of a dam in 1852. The level of the water was raised some 12 feet creating a lake that first was called Carp Lake, now known as Lake Leelanau.

The State of Michigan constructed one of its fine harbors here, and Leland is an ideal place from which to start cruising the north end of Lake Michigan. The Leland harbor may be approached safely from the north, south or west, but the harbor itself must be entered from the south. There is a flashing red light on a white column at the south end of the breakwater. Care must be taken in proceeding north up the channel into the marina because there is often a sandbar build-up off the end of the inner breakwater. After passing the south end of the outer breakwater favor the left-hand side of the channel into the marina. The dockmaster's shack is located just on the right, adjacent to the gas dock. The Leland harbor, incidentally, is designated as a harbor of refuge.

Full facilities are available at dockside: gas and diesel fuel, ice, water, electricity, and pump-out. It is only a short walk up the street from the dock for shopping. Along the Carp River is a strip once known as "Fish Town;" the former fishermen's shanties have been converted into quaint specialty shops. Carlson's Fisheries sell fine fresh and smoked fish; there is a bakery which makes excellent croissants; several ice cream stores; and up the street further, a supermarket which also carries a full line of alcoholic beverages. The Standard Oil station can take care of most mechanical problems. There is no laundry in town, however. On rainy days try a visit to the nearby library.

Here's a personal hint: try some of the smoked chubs from Carlson's. They saved the life of one of my crewmates several years ago. He had spent the entire crossing of Lake Michigan with his head in a bucket. When we reached quiet water, he curbed his hunger with three of those chubs washed down with beer.

The Bluebird Restaurant has facilities for both formal and informal dining as does the Falling Waters Lodge on the Carp River, and the Leland Lodge will provide pick-up service at the dock for dining in its scenic restaurant.

There are fine beaches along the shore, both north and

South Manitou Island   *Robert T. McCoy photo*

Here's A Real Beauty *Michigan Travel Bureau photo*

SUMMER SAIL II

south of the marina.

No visit to Leland would be complete without crossing over to South Manitou Island which is part of Sleeping Bear Dunes National Lakeshore Park. There is a fine harbor on the east shore of the island, protected from all but east or southeast blows. But there are no dock facilities, so you must dinghy ashore. In anchoring, the harbor is deep, except close to shore a narrow shelf of 20-foot depth extends out from the sand beach for a distance of from 50 to 150 feet. Anchor here in such a way that you will not drag anchor into the deeper water or in an easterly wind end up with your stern on the beach.

A trip ashore is well worthwhile. The National Park Service is maintaining both islands as wilderness areas, so no vehicles are allowed. But there are fine hiking trails and interesting things to see. There is a restaurant a short distance from the ferry dock (operating from Leland in season). A visitor center has been established in the old island post office, and exhibits tell the human and natural history of the island. The old Coast Guard station is now the residence of the Park Service rangers who also supervise the lighthouse. The western shore of the island has high sand hills offering spectacular views out over the big lake, and near the southwestern corner of the island is the Valley of the Giants, a grove of virgin white cedar trees which somehow escaped the lumberman's axe. The world record white cedar is located in the grove. It measures 17.6 feet in circumference and stands 113 feet tall. A total of 528 growth rings were counted on one of the fallen trees in the grove.

South Manitou is the southernmost of an island chain that extends north all the way to the Straits of Mackinac. North Manitou was acquired by the National Park Service in 1984 and is undeveloped. There is a dangerous shoal area off the south end of North Manitou which must be given wide berth when heading back to Leland or to the north. It is marked by a flashing red buoy. After clearing this shoal, a heading of 50 degrees will clear Cat Head Point.

Departing from Leland head due north at least three miles before turning northeast. And that's where we now will head.

World Record White Cedar — South Manitou Island
Fitzgerald photo

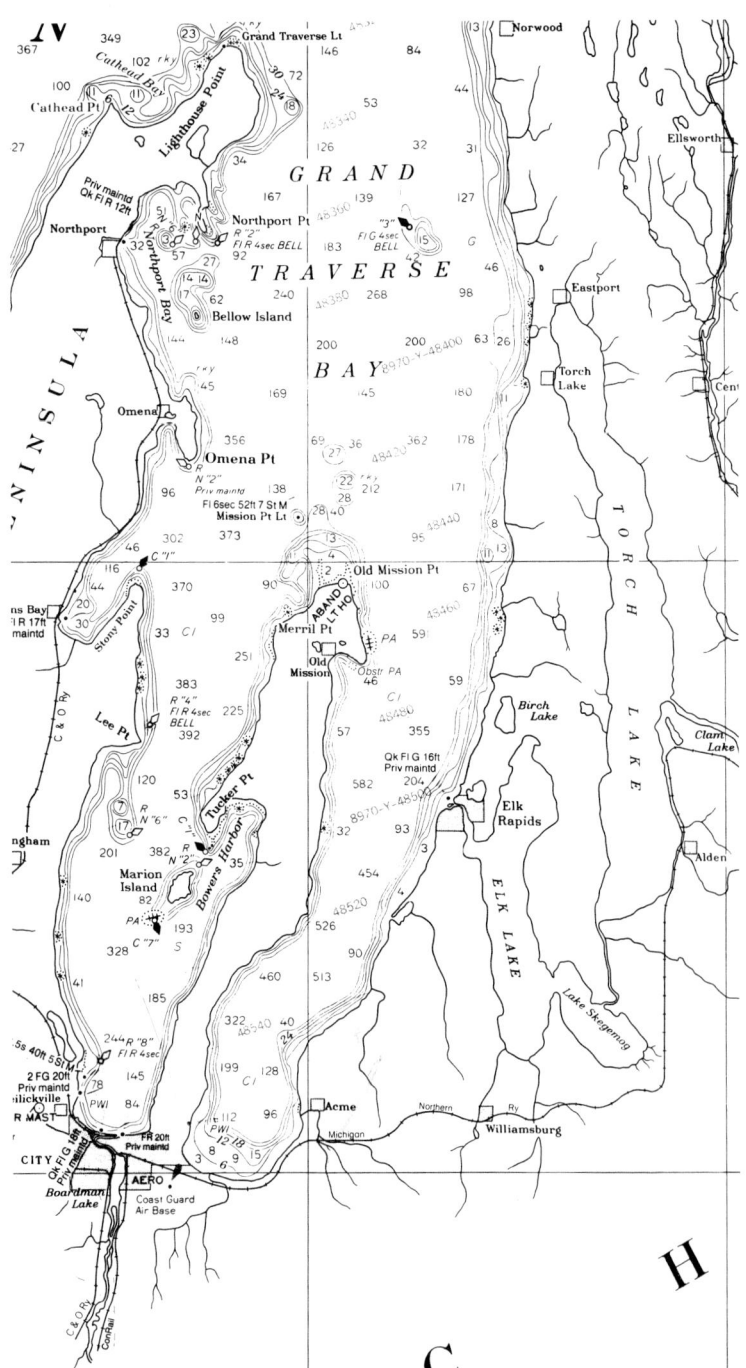

4

GRAND TRAVERSE BAY

There is no mystery as to how Grand Traverse Bay got its name. The French *courier du bois* coasting south along this shore of Lake Michigan came to the mouth of a large bay and had to leave the coast to cross it. They called it *le grande traverse*, in English, Grand Traverse.

The bay extends almost 35 miles north to south and is a little over 10 miles across at its widest point. It is divided into two arms by the Mission Point Peninsula.

The area was the exclusive domain of the Ottawa and Chippewa Indian tribes until the middle of the 19th century. They being somewhat warlike tribes, development of the fur trade was discouraged in this area in contrast to the other shore of the lake, particularly the Green Bay area.

Recorded history begins in 1839 with the appearance

of Protestant missionaries on the peninsula, locating first at what is now Old Mission. The verdant forests of pine and hardwoods soon attracted development, and the first sawmill was built at the head of West Bay in 1847. A settlement developed there which became Traverse City. By 1875 there were 15 sawmills in the area, and the lumber cut was estimated at 25 million feet that year. By 1893 the estimated production was close to 250 million board feet. Grand Traverse Bay provided excellent protection for the schooners which carried the lumber to Chicago and other ports in southern Lake Michigan.

The lumber industry tailed off in the early part of the 20th century, and farmers took to homesteading the area with potatoes being one crop which did well in the sandy soil. It was the discovery of the land's suitability for cherry trees, however, which brought the next economic boom. This area of Michigan is now the largest producer of red tart cherries in the country, dwarfing the production in Door County across the lake.

About the time the first orchards were planted a handful of Chicagoans learned they could escape the heat of the city during the summer by moving to the Grand Traverse Bay region where the prevailing winds were washed clean of pollen, dust, and heat as they moved across the broad expanse of Lake Michigan. Many built summer homes here and became established summer residents. In addition to the climate are the scenery; the hundreds of inland lakes, rivers, and rills — all filled with fish — and the mile after mile of sand beaches kissed only gently by the summer sun. All of these lured vacationists until now the summer resort industry is the second most important in the area's economy.

Most tourists arrive by auto, and as a matter of fact, the area is more easily visited by road than it is by water. It is a good day's sail from Lake Michigan to Traverse City, and the shores of the bay are rocky and generally should not be approached closer than a half mile. All points and spits should be given even more leeway.

For those who do make the trip by water there are two fine marinas at Traverse City. The recommended one is Harbor West in Greilickville which is the harbor of refuge for this area and which offers protection in all weather for either anchoring or docking. Approaching from the north stay east of the lighted buoy R6 as there are shoals between the shore and this buoy. Harbor West is just beyond this buoy (2800 feet to be exact) on a heading of 239 degrees. The entrance is marked by flashing red and green lights. Full facilities are offered, including a 40-ton marine derrick. Fuel, electricity, water, ice, restrooms, and showers in the clubhouse are available, and there is a public beach nearby. Transportation to downtown Traverse City is easily arranged.

The downtown marina, the Dunkin L. Clinch Yacht Harbor, is another mile and a half southwest. The entrance is marked by a flashing green light on an 18-foot pole. Again full services are available, and downtown Traverse City is only several blocks away. Traverse City is a bustling community with fine shops and restaurants, hospital, library, museum, etc. It is the major metropolis for this entire resort area.

In East Bay the beach of "sugar sand" is known as the Miracle Mile, and many of the unique shops and restaurants can be visited during a walk along the beach. Just up from the marina is the Park Hotel with a restaurant on the top floor. Other recommended eateries are the Waterfront Inn and the century-old Bowers Harbor Inn at Old Mission. If you are interested in a day ashore a new Jack Nicklaus golf course opened at Grand

Traverse City — Downtown *Robert T. McCoy photo*

Traverse City — Harbor West   *Robert T. McCoy photo*

SUMMER SAIL II   **47**

Traverse Resort in 1984.

There are a number of other interesting harbors to visit in Grand Traverse Bay, enough as a matter of fact to make up a mini-cruise in itself.

On the east shore of the bay is Elk Rapids, a community of about 1,300 souls, which has a very nice marina. The entrance to the harbor basin is marked by range boards, the range being 160 degrees true of the center of the channel between the breakwaters. There is shallow water on the north side of the southern breakwater. Three red buoys mark the edge of the channel to starboard. The harbor is capable of handling boats up to 60 feet in length. Fuel and electricity are available at the marina which also has a harbor house with lounge room, restrooms, and showers. During the boating season this facility is available 24 hours a day. The Elk Rapids shopping area is adjacent to the harbor, with a bank, stores, and all services.

Over on the northeast corner of the Mission Peninsula there is an anchorage available at Old Mission Bay which offers protection from all winds except southeast. There are no lights or aids to navigation, but the bay is deep along the the northeast shore. The west shore is shallow and cannot be approached closer than 1,500 feet. Use of the lead is recommended.

On the east shore of the west arm of the bay is Bowers Harbor about 10 miles north of Traverse City. There are no docks available, but the harbor is deep and secure. Anchorage is available but only close to shore.

More inviting is Suttons Bay, a large bay inside Suttons Point, on the west shore of the west arm, terminating at the community of Suttons Bay. Coming from the north a course of 220 degrees will take you right down the center of the bay. Coming from the south, stay east of Lee Point, marked by lighted red bell buoy #4. A green can #1 marks the northerly end of Suttons Point Shoal which must be rounded before proceeding south into Suttons Bay.

There is good anchorage anywhere in the bay with protection from all winds except northeast. The Suttons Bay public dock has 5 feet of water (LWD). Gasoline and diesel fuel are available at the dock along with electricity and water. There are two restaurants and a store at Suttons Bay, and More's Market will deliver groceries.

Another good anchorage and small marina are available about six miles north of Suttons Bay at New Mission Bay, also called Omena Bay. There is good water with secure holding anywhere in this bay, and the Omena Yacht Club is located in the northeast corner of the bay with 10 feet of water at its dock. Food and general supplies are available, but gasoline can be had only at a nearby service station.

The most popular harbor in Grand Traverse Bay is at Northport on the northeast corner of the Leelanau Peninsula. This is an excellent harbor to visit on your way north or south along the shore of Lake Michigan.

The entrance to Northport Bay is about six miles south of Lighthouse Point, where Grand Traverse Light is located. The southeasterly tip of Northport Point is marked by red lighted bell buoy #2, and this must be given some room when rounding to the south. Off to the port side Bellow Island will appear. After rounding buoy R2, head directly west, giving room to red nun #4 and then red nun #6. The harbor entrance is marked by flashing red and green lights, and the marina is to port after passing through the breakwaters.

Approaching Northport from the south, stand at least 2,000 feet off shore in passing New Mission Point. From that point a course due north will put you on a heading for

Elk Rapids   *Robert T. McCoy photo*

Suttons Bay *Michigan Waterways Commission photo*

Northport *Robert T. McCoy photo*

Northport Point red bell buoy #2. This course will take you 1,500 feet east of Bellow Island, and stay at least 1,000 feet off the island because there are several reefs north and northwest of the island. Once well clear of the island and just short of buoy #2, proceed west into the harbor, leaving red nuns #4 and #6 to starboard.

Anchorage is poor in Northport harbor, but the municipal marina, expanded in 1959 with the help of the Michigan Waterways Commission, has a large basin with a minimum of 8 feet of water and docks for 90 boats, with some slips 60 feet long. Electricity, pump-out, and water are available, with fuel by delivery. The dock is part of a municipal park which includes bathing beach, playground equipment, picnic area, and toilet facilities with showers; all in all a well-serviced marina.

A general store, two grocery stores, drugstore, liquor store, hardware store, bakery, automatic laundry, and four restaurants are nearby. Digger's Den features spectacular views and fresh whitefish. Ice is available at the general store. There is also a hospital and medical services in town. As I said previously, Northport is an ideal stopping-off place on any cruise of this shore of Lake Michigan, lying about midway between the harbors at Leland and Charlevoix.

Actually a fine week's cruise can be encompassed entirely within Grand Traverse Bay. It is particularly attractive to gunkholers. One night could be spent at Elk Rapids on the east arm, then an anchorage at Old Mission Harbor, around the peninsula into the west arm with anchorage at Bowers Harbor, a visit to Traverse City at either of its two marinas, then a night at Suttons Bay, another at Omena Bay, winding up at Northport.

If this doesn't fit your time frame, however, we will make *le grande traverse* and proceed to Charlevoix.

Dahlia Shoal
248
199
59
Good Hart
R MAST & R RELAY TR
247
52
Seven Mile Pt
217
199
37
157
169
169
Harbor Springs
Little Traverse Lt
Fl G 7.5sec 72ft 14 St M
Oden
Conway
Crooked
Round Lake
177
121
175
208
91
187
LITTLE TRAVERSE BAY
Bay View
283
240
Depth over Crib 26 ft
91
169
151
Fl R 2.5sec 44ft 5 St M
PETOSKEY
31
31
224
352
31
34
Big Rock Pt
STACK
Nine Mile Pt
Bayshore
STACKS
R MAST
Bear Creek
254
HORN
FR 41ft 12 St M
Fl R 4sec 24ft
Priv maintd
R "2"
Fl R 4s BELL
228
South Pt
TANK
CG
AERO
STACK
SILO
47
CHARLEVOIX
Susan Lake
LAKE CHARLEVOIX
Horton Bay
Walloon Lake
Clarion
Walloon Lake
Ironton
ConRail
Advance
Boyne City
Boyne Valley R R
Ellsworth
East Jordan
Eastport
Torch Lake
Central Lake
Intermediate Lake
TORCH
Bellaire
C & O Ry

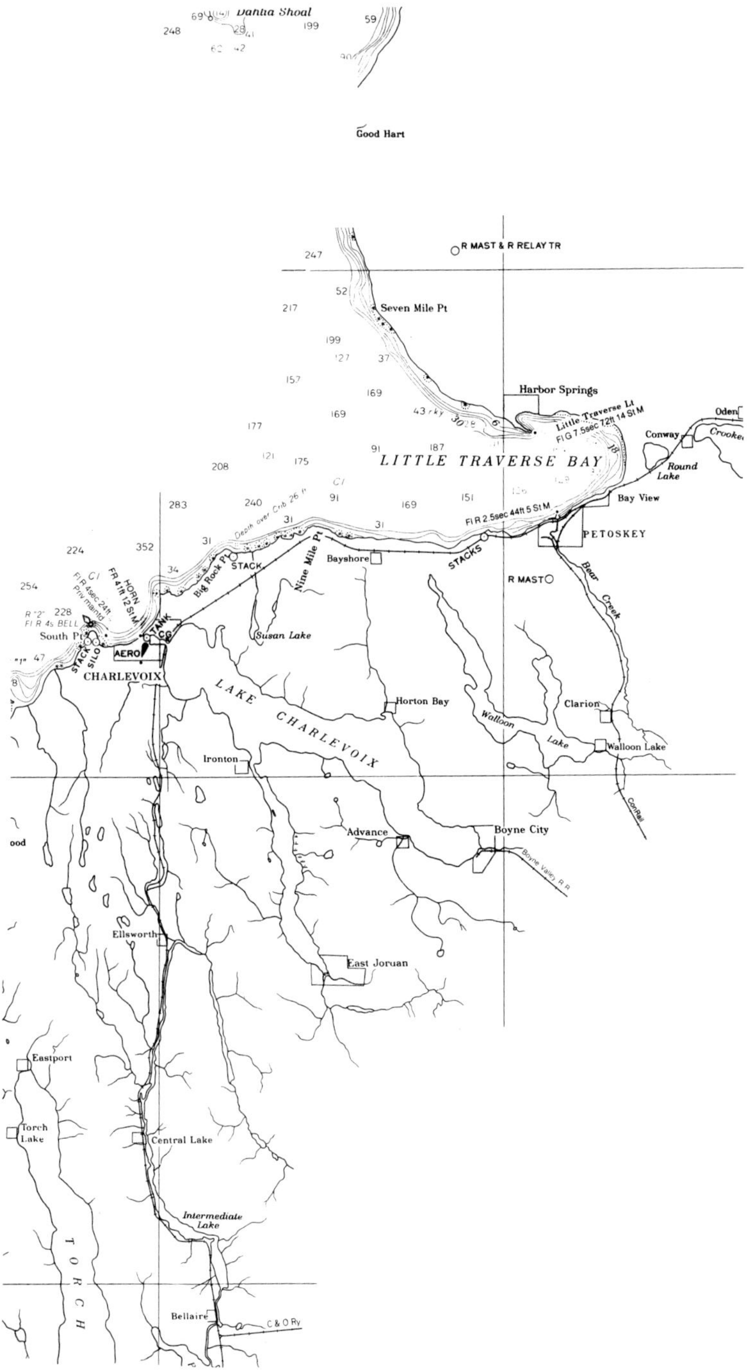

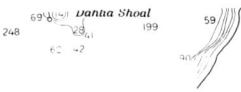

5

CHARLEVOIX THE BEAUTIFUL

Charlevoix the Beautiful it is called. And rightly so.

This resort village at the mouth of the Pine River about midway up the rounding shore between Little and Grand Traverse Bays deserves a stop of at least several days on any cruise of northern Lake Michigan.

The tall stacks of a cement plant southwest of the city can be seen for 15 to 20 miles away. (There are also stacks northeast of the city which are actually closer to Petoskey but can still be seen as you enter Charlevoix. These are not to be confused with the aforementioned stacks.) There are some rocky points both north and south of the harbor, so the approach must be made from the north or west on course from 100 degrees to 200 degrees. There is an unnamed promontory one and one-half miles north/-northeast from the entrance, locally called North Point.

Charlevoix — From Lake Michigan   *Robert T. McCoy photo*

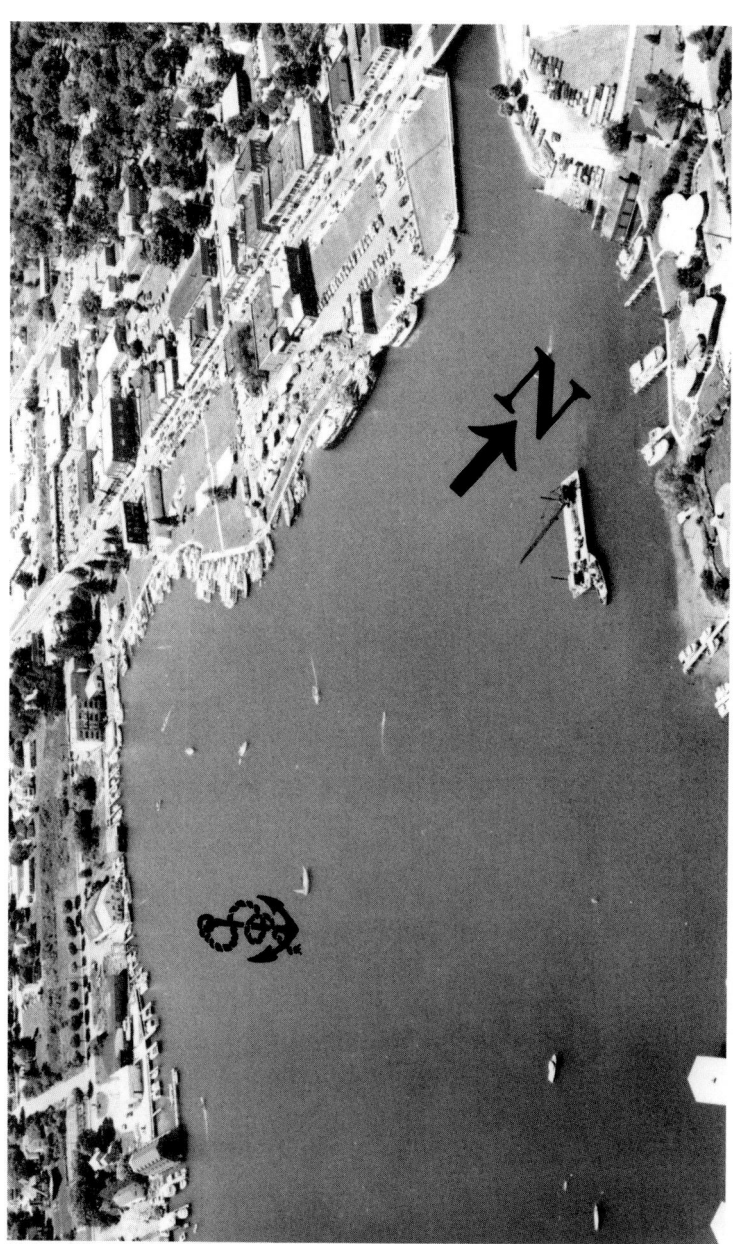

Charlevoix Harbor Robert T. McCoy photo

SUMMER SAIL II

Boats should stay at least 3,000 feet offshore to clear underwater boulders in that area. South Point is another rocky promontory one and three-quarters miles to the west, also requiring a wide berth. South Point is marked with a red bell buoy #2 with a flashing white light.

Entrance to the harbor is through twin pierheads into the Pine River. The north pierhead is marked by a flashing white light on a white tower 61 feet high; the south pierhead a flashing red light on a white tower 41 feet high. The river passes under a highway bridge which opens on the hour and half-hour for exactly five minutes. There is often a current in the river moving in or out according to the winds, and it may run as high as three miles an hour if it is flowing from the lake into the river; so skippers need to exert due caution so as not to be driven into the bridge. The bulkheads on each side are steel revetments, and there are holding cleats provided; but skippers must be prepared to slow boats sufficiently so a crewman can get ashore and tie up.

Once through the bridge you are in beautiful Round Lake, the main harbor for downtown Charlevoix. The lake is about 2,000 feet in diameter, and while anchoring is permitted, it is not adviseable inasmuch as the bottom is weedy and there is not sufficient room to let out enough scope to provide uneventful anchorage.

The municipal marina is to starboard upon entering the lake, and while there are a number of slips for transient yachts, they are often filled. The dockmaster monitors channel 16 and will advise you as to the availability of slips or alternate docking arrangements. There has been considerable construction of new docking facilities in the area in recent years, and other private marinas are available both in Round Lake and on into Lake Charlevoix. The latter is entered directly from Round Lake by an extension of the Pine River, and no bridge is involved. To starboard upon entering Lake Charlevoix is the Irish Boat Shop and Marina which is a facility of considerable capacity, and there are other private docks nearby which accept transients.

Good anchorage is available in Lake Charlevoix, particularly along the west shore about three-quarters of a mile south of the channel from Round Lake. Sailors with dinghies may find that it is preferable to anchor in this area and dinghy ashore.

The Village of Charlevoix is a charming resort center which has been popular with people from the Chicago area, southern Michigan, and Indiana for many years. The name of the community comes from the French missionary, Pierre du Charlevoix, who explored this area as early as 1721. The first permanent settler did not arrive until the mid-19th century, however; 1854 to be exact. Lumbering and fishing were the initial occupations, but it began to develop into a resort center in the 1870s.

Swimming and sunning are probably the most popular outdoor sports during the summer months, and there are three supervised beaches available, two of them on Lake Charlevoix and the third on Lake Michigan just south of the pierheads. There is excellent sport fishing. The Michigan Department of Natural Resources has called Charlevoix "the lake trout capital of the world." Charter boats are available.

Possibly though the real charm lies in such informal activities as watching the draw bridge go up and down for the passing of a beautiful sloop, collecting driftwood and Petoskey stones along the beaches, listening to a band concert in East Park, or just watching the sun disappear into Lake Michigan in the evening.

There are a number of charming shops in the village,

Pine River Bridge — Charlevoix
Michigan Travel Bureau photo

Charming Shops In Charlevoix
Michigan Travel Bureau photo

some of them featuring fudge or chocolate cookies. Also there are a number of fine supper clubs and restaurants, specifically Grey Gables on the shore of Lake Charlevoix; Riccardo's, an Italian restaurant overlooking the Pine River; and Duffy's, a mile north on the highway, which will provide transportation.

Up the walk from the public marina is the Chamber of Commerce office, and the staff is happy to provide information on where to go and what to see in the area. Across the street is Oleson's Market, and nearby are a fine bakery and a fresh fish market. There are several restaurants right in the downtown area.

Charlevoix is the home port of the Coast Guard cutter *Sundew*. The town also has a hatchery and rearing station, operated by the U.S. Fish and Wildlife Service, where hundreds of thousands of lake trout are reared each year for restocking the Great Lakes. It is also the home port for the launch *Beaver Islander* which carries passengers to Beaver Island and back.

Charlevoix is also known as "Hemingway Land" since Ernest Hemingway spent many summers in the area as a young man and incorporated many of the area scenes into his writing. Visitors may be interested in the Greensky Hill Church east of the city on Highway 31. With its adjacent burial ground it is completely Indian, and the hundred-year-old hand-hewn plank pews of the original structure are still in use and in excellent condition, as are the huge exterior logs. The church is named for the Rev. Peter Greensky, a Methodist who settled in this area in the early 19th century.

Also nearby is the noted Interlochen Music School, and public concerts are offered during the summer season.

A visit to Charlevoix is not complete without a sail on beautiful Lake Charlevoix itself. It is some 14 miles long, and there are two quaint resort communities at each end of its eastern arms. One is Boyne City where a new city dock is located in Memorial Park at the foot of State Street. Slips will accommodate boats up to 60 feet; electricity and water are available; and gas and diesel fuel by truck delivery. It is an easy walk into the village whose downtown has undergone a complete revamp, and there are grocery store, ice, marine service, medical facilities, and restaurants close by.

The other arm of Lake Charlevoix extends south to another small port at East Jordan, a beautiful, quiet harbor. The dock has electricity and water; gas and diesel will be delivered; and also groceries. There are several gourmet restaurants: The Jordan Inn (reservations only), Ken's Anchorage, Ridge Racquet Club, and the Wagon Wheel. Lake and stream fishing are available with local guides. You can shoot deer, ducks, and a variety of wild birds with your camera in Sportsmen's Park, and there are canoe float trips down the Jordan River.

There are only two potential water problems in Lake Charlevoix. There is a sandbar off Horse Point about two miles northwest of Boyne City, shown on the chart. And when proceeding into the south arm, there is a cable ferry crossing, also on the chart, which poses a problem while the ferry is in operation. Otherwise, no problems and there is a place called the Landing at the east end of the ferry line where you can get excellent hamburgers.

The people of Charlevoix are very friendly and display a brand of hospitality that is equalled in very few places. They are very proud of their community and rightfully so because, as their desciptive name — Charlevoix the Beautiful — implies, Charlevoix is indeed a very beautiful community. It is made so by millions of petunias, in all colors of the rainbow, lining many of their streets and

Boyne City　　　　　　　　　　　*Robert T. McCoy photo*

East Jordan Robert T. McCoy photo

SUMMER SAIL II

adorning all kinds of imaginable places.

To further enhance Charlevoix as a must stop on your cruise of this shore of Lake Michigan, the people of Charlevoix warmly invite everyone to visit them by presenting a variety of community events aimed directly at their thousands of summer visitors. In May they have a fishing tournament of sorts that presents more to do than fishing. In July, the last week to be precise, the Annual Venetian Festival is held. This gala event dates back to 1931. August has the Waterfront Art Fair that was begun in 1959 and where artists from all over the Midwest display their works. For those who have put their boats in storage for the winter by early October and for land-lubbers who appreciate Nature's autumn parade of colors but who would like to see it from a different view other than a touring car, there are the Annual Color Cruises to Beaver Island during the first two weekends of October.

Given all these amenities, the visiting yachtsman can well spend two to five days in the Charlevoix area at almost any time of the season.

Public Marina — Charlevoix   *Michigan Travel Bureau photo*

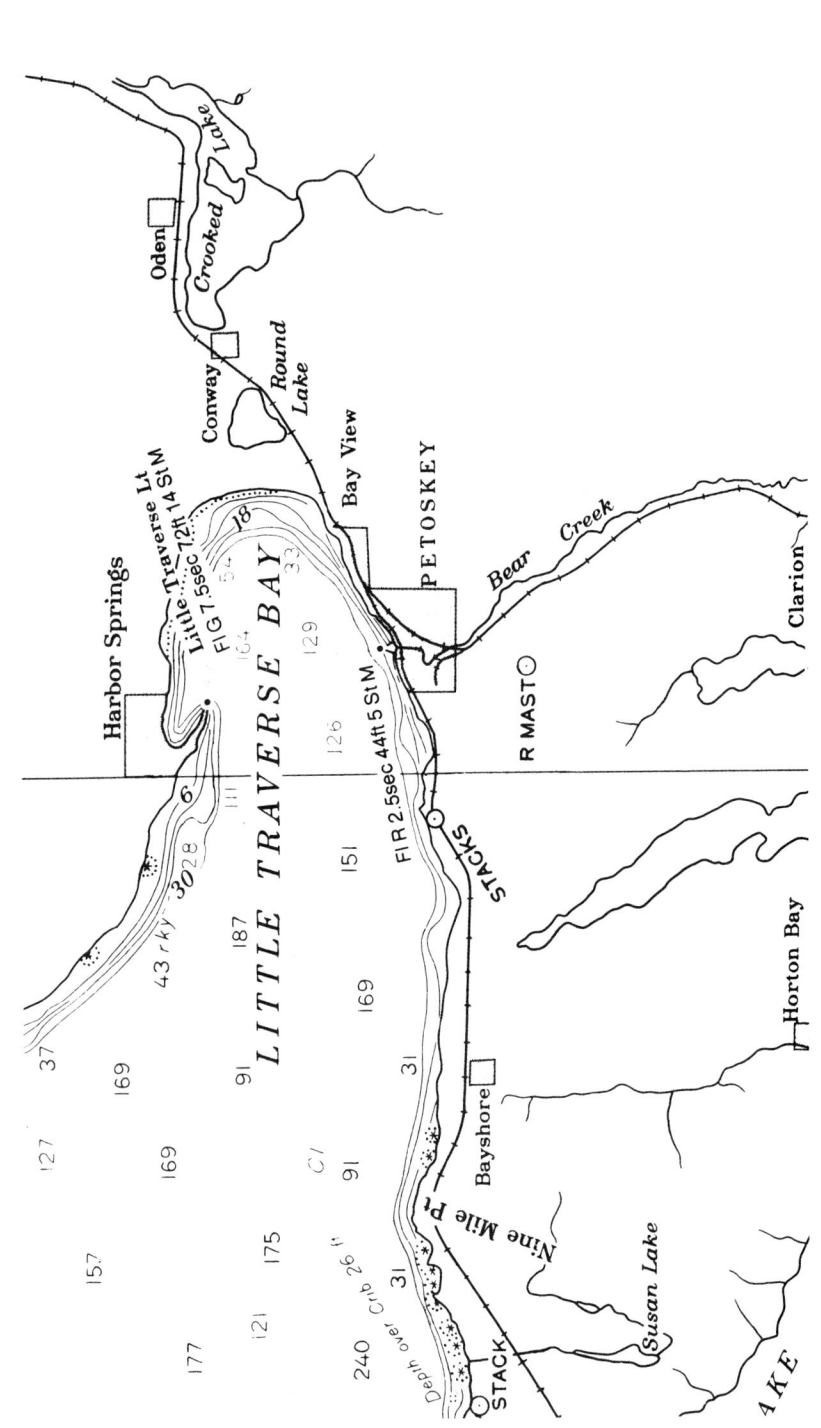

6

LITTLE TRAVERSE BAY

The resort community of Petoskey is one of many such communities whose name is derived from its early Indian history. The area around Little Traverse Bay was the home of Ottawas for may generations before the coming of the white man. One of the first settlers of the harbor at the mouth of the Bear River in Little Traverse Bay was an Indian family by the name of Pe-te-se-gah. He and his wife and fourteen children settled there in 1830, and the name Petoskey is an English corruption of that Indian name.

More Indians followed Ignace Petoskey to the area, and in 1851 a Protestant missionary established an Indian school there. The teacher at the school, Andrew Porter, acted as postmaster of the territory and erected mailboxes at the school building which were labeled "mail going south" and "mail going north." At first the mail was carried by Indians on foot, then on horseback. The mailboxes are still intact at the mission building.

The area was opened to white settlement in the 1870s after treaties with the Indians expired, and the extension of the railroad to Petoskey in 1875 ignited further settlement in the area. One of the early industries was the conversion of limestone in kilns into lime.

The community matured rapidly from that time forward, and the beginnings of the tourist business were noticeable by the end of the 19th century.

Petoskey is now the metropolis of this very lush resort area and as such is well worth the yachtsman's visit.

Little Traverse Bay is wide open with plenty of deep water. There is some shoal water on both the north and south shores, but if the navigator holds off from 1,800 to 2,000 feet he should encounter no trouble.

The municipal dock is protected on the west by a government breakwater which projects out from shore about 1220 feet. There is a flashing red light and a red triangular day mark on a white skeleton tower near the end of the breakwater. The Pen-Dixy Cement Corp. wharf, a commercial dock about 1100 feet long, lies three miles westerly from Petoskey harbor and should not be confused with the government breakwater. There are about 70 slips available in the marina with water depths ranging from 16 feet at the outer end to 6 feet at the end of the last docks. All services are available: telephone, water, electricity, fuel and garbage service, pump-out, restrooms, and showers. As a matter of fact, the Petoskey marina consistently receives high marks for its personnel and the condition and maintenance of its facilities.

The harbormaster stands by on channel 16 and works 9 and 68. There is 24-hour security in the marina which is open from Memorial Day into September.

A unique gaslight shopping district is two blocks uptown from the harbor. The city sits on a hillside sloping down to the water, adding to its attractiveness.

The Country Lantern offers both inside and outside dining. The Candlelight specializes in prime rib and fresh fish. And in neighboring Bay View are the Bay View Inn and the Terrace Inn; both highly recommended.

Petoskey is known as the "City of Million Dollar Sunsets." The first time it was so labelled was by a reporter for the Grand Rapids *Times* in 1873. The title refers to the beautiful vista to the west across Little Traverse Bay and Lake Michigan, affording a spectacular view of the summer sunsets over the lake.

Just to the east of Petoskey is another well known resort community: Bay View. It was founded back in the 19th century as a Methodist church summer campground and became a prized summer resort area when local interests financed the extension of the railroad line from Petoskey east to Bay View.

As a matter of fact, the whole eastern shore of Little Traverse Bay, extending north and then west to Harbor Springs, is one of the wealthiest summer resort areas in all of Lower Michigan.

Harbor Springs lies just across Little Traverse Bay, four miles north of Petoskey. This well-protected harbor offers security in any weather and can accommodate the largest vessels on the Great Lakes. It is protected on the west and south by Harbor Point which extends almost a mile out from shore. There is a flashing green light on a white skeleton tower at the end of Harbor Point which is visible for about 14 miles.

There are ample docking facilities plus a fine mooring area inside Harbor Point. In addition to the municipal marina at the west end of the harbor, there is also the Irish

Petoskey

Robert T. McCoy photo

Harbor Springs *Robert T. McCoy photo*

Boat Shop Marina and another privately operated marina, the Walstrom Marina, to the east.

The harbor has a good holding ground for anchoring. Bottoms are sand and clay. If anchoring in the middle of the harbor, be prepared to use a good length of anchor rode and do not anchor in the course from the point to the docks as there is considerable traffic. Look out also for race buoys as there are about a dozen 5-foot high spars scattered about the harbor.

The city docks consist of one 400-foot dock with slips, plus slips along a bulkhead for 400 feet east of the dock, and a 100-foot steel pile dock at the far east end. Boats up to 65 feet can be accommodated in some of the slips. Water around the dock varies from 6 feet at the shore to 16 feet at the ends. Information about dock spaces can be obtained from the dockmaster working channel 9. Fuel, garbage disposal, water, electricity, ice, pump-out, restrooms, and showers are available.

Dock spaces are also available at the Irish Boat Shop and Walstrom Marina, and both provide all marine services. All other docks in the harbor are private.

Harbor Springs has been a noted summer resort for many years, and a large variety of distinctly individualized shops and restaurants are available. As an example of this unique quality, Between The Covers Bookstore has a rear terrace for readers. There are also golf courses and tennis courts nearby.

Recommended restaurants are Staffords on the waterfront for seafood; the Water's Edge, specializing in Beef Wellington and Chicken Audrey; plus Juillerets; the New York; the Harbor Pier; and the Colonial Inn.

There has been considerable trouble with excessive wakes causing damage to docks, small craft, and property on shore, both on Harbor Point as well as on the north side of the harbor. The harbor is under constant patrol by the sheriff's department and the city marine patrol, generally in a marked Boston Whaler, and NO WAKE regulations are strictly enforced.

The Harbor Springs Yacht Club sponsors a large regatta on the weekend after the conclusion of the Chicago-Mackinac Race, with many of the racers from that event returning to Harbor Springs to participate. The dock spaces generally are crowded on that particular weekend, normally the last weekend in July.

Both Harbor Springs and Petoskey are beautifully equipped marinas, and both resort communities are most attractive for the visiting sailor. No cruise in northern Lake Michigan is complete without a visit to at least one of these harbors.

For those with smaller craft and who are interested in a unique side-trip, there is an inland waterway in northern Michigan, relatively unknown to most of the boating public, which is one of the finest cruising waterways in the Midwest. The 40-mile route is located 25 miles south of the Mackinac Bridge and traverses the tip of the Lower Peninsula from Lake Michigan to Lake Huron. It is available to boats up to 30 feet in length drawing less than 5 feet.

The waterway begins in Crooked Lake, its most southernly point, which is about eight miles north of Petoskey and Harbor Springs. It connects through the Crooked River with Burt Lake to Indian River and then Mullet Lake. From there sailors enter the Cheboygan River and then travel on out to Lake Huron.

The route was first used more than a hundred years ago by Indian canoes as a shortcut from Lake Huron to Lake Michigan. A large sandbar was removed from the head of the Indian River back in 1874, making the route navigable to larger boats. During the lumbering era, the system of lakes and rivers was used extensively for transporting forest products and supplying the lumber camps. At the turn of the century, small steam-powered excursion boats carried tourists from the western shore of Crooked Lake to a resort hotel on Mullet Lake.

Since then the inland waterway has become one of the most popular small boat trips in the area. The U.S. Corps of Engineers dredged the river channels to about 5 feet in depth and 30 feet wide in the late 1950s, and the waterway is still maintained by the Corps.

The waterway represents some of the most scenic and safe cruising anywhere in the Great Lakes area, and it is particularly beautiful in the fall, splendid with Mother nature's colors.

Riding The Spinnaker *Michigan Travel Bureau photo*

JAMES J. STRANG
(FROM THE ONLY PHOTOGRAPH OF HIM KNOWN TO BE IN EXISTENCE).

7

THE STORY OF KING STRANG

Before we continue north to the Beaver Island group, let me digress to tell the story of James Jesse Strang, the Mormon prophet who led his flock to Beaver Island in the 1850s, had himself proclaimed king of the island, was twice elected to the Michigan Legislature, and was then assassinated by two disgruntled members of his commune. A visit to Beaver Island is much more enjoyable if you are familiar with this story.

Let me begin by quoting from a booklet entitled *King Strang* written by Robert P. Weeks, published by the Five Wives Press of Ann Arbor, Michigan and available in area bookstores. Weeks is an English professor at the University of Michigan and has a summer home on Beaver Island.

"Although kings have never done well in the United

States, we have a keen interest in them. This goes far to explain our infatuation with Jesse Strang, the Mormon prophet who reigned over an island kingdom in northern Lake Michigan for half a dozen years in the late 1850s. But it only begins to explain the endearing appeal which Strang's story has had for a wide variety of readers for whom it has been told for more than a century.

"Strang was much more than a mere monarch, he was a widely improbable mixture. He was a fiery opponent of polygamy who when he died left five wives — four of them pregnant; he was a divinely chosen prophet of God who was the political boss of two counties and was in the state legislature; an harsh narrow puritan who wore a crimson robe and jewelled crown and was attended by a retinue of viceroys, chevaliers, and other feudal nobles with splendid titles."

Picture, if you will, a man who was barely 5'3", of slight build but with a full beard, curiously bulging forehead, and intense, deeply set dark eyes, giving him a dramatic presence that compensated, along with a black stovepipe hat, for his short stature.

Strang grew up in western New York state at a time of deep religious ferment. It was during this period that an angel with the odd name of Moroni had appeared in the bedroom of a farmhouse in that area to tell a 17-year-old farm boy that additional books to the Bible, dealing with the Lost Tribes of Israel and written on golden plates, were buried in a nearby hill. Young Joseph Smith dug up the plates, translated them as *The Book of Mormon*, and became founder of the Church of Jesus Christ of Latter-Day Saints. It was some twenty years later when Strang first met Smith. Strang had become a lawyer and migrated to Burlington, Wisconsin to set up his practice. His wife's sister was a devout Mormon, and through this connection

Strang journeyed to Nauvoo, Illinois where Smith had set up a Mormon community. Strang was converted to Mormonism and baptised by Smith himself.

At the time, the Mormon community at Nauvoo was under intense pressure from the citizenry of the surrounding area, which seethed with violent anti-Mormon feelings. Strang proposed to Smith that he found a Mormon community near Burlington, and Smith promptly made him an elder of the church and urged him to do so. Strang founded his community at a place which he named Voree.

It was only a matter of months, however, when Joseph Smith was assassinated by a mob in Carthage, Illinois.

Several startling things occurred to Strang within the next few weeks. At the precise moment when Smith was shot to death, Strang was taking a solitary walk through the countryside outside Burlington, and as he said later, he heard celestial music, looked into the sky and saw an angel accompanied by heavenly hosts glide down into the meadow in which he stood. The angel stretched forth a hand, annointing Strang's head with oil, a sign that henceforth, Prophet Strang was to be supreme ruler of the Saints on earth.

Some two weeks later, he received a letter postmarked Nauvoo, Illinois, June 19, 1844. The letter had supposedly been written by Joseph Smith nine days before his assassination, and in it he endorsed Strang's idea of a new colony in Wisconsin and appointed Strang his successor.

Strang exploited the letter to the fullest. He called it documentary proof of the legitimacy of his claim to leadership of the Mormon church vis-a-vis Brigham Young who had staked a counter-claim in Nauvoo.

Strang exhibited the letter in all principal cities from

the Mississippi River to the Atlantic. He wrote in 1854 that "in all that region, a hundred thousand witnesses are ready to bear testimony."

Young branded the letter "a wicked forgery cooked up by a bald-faced liar."

Not surprisingly, Strang soon received the holy word under remarkably similar circumstances to that of his predecessor. He was again visited by an angel who told him that he was to receive *The Book of the Law of the Lord.* He was instructed to dig at a precise spot and led four of his disciples there, standing apart as they commenced to dig. They chopped their way through the roots of an oak tree and finally came upon three brass plates.

When Joseph Smith had dug up his buried plates in upstate New York, he allowed no one to witness the event, although later several people swore they had seen them. But Strang showed his to his awed followers, went into seclusion for a week to translate the strange marks on them, later reporting that they consisted of certain "lost Levantine languages." He said that the plates were a record left by a Rajah Manchore of Vorito, an Oriental potentate who milleniums ago had ruled a godlike people on the Wisconsin frontier, now leveled to dust but destined one day to rise again.

From Smith's death until 1847 Strang waged a vigorous campaign to succeed the dead prophet as leader of the Church of Jesus Christ of Latter-Day Saints. But by this time Brigham Young had led his disciples west to their present location in Utah. And the natives were getting restless around Strang's community in Wisconsin.

On a trip by steamer from Buffalo back to Milwaukee, Strang had observed a group of beautiful islands off the western shore of Michigan. In the spring of 1847 Strang and four Mormons from Voree visited the islands. The largest of the group, Big Beaver, is 13 miles long and 6 miles wide. It has broad white sand beaches the length of its eastern shore and sand dunes and bluffs along the western side. At the northern end is one of the finest sheltered harbors in the Great Lakes. And the island is in the midst of what was and remains today one of the best fishing areas in the lakes. All in all, it was an ideal spot for a Utopian community.

At the appropriate time the prophet announced that he had been visited by an angel who instructed him to move his colony to "a land amid wide waters and covered with large timber, with a deep broad bay on one side."

For the next several years Mormons streamed to Beaver Island where they found a virgin wilderness. They blessed the rivers, lakes, bays, and hills with proper biblical names; they cleared the fields and planted; layed out a network of roads; and erected sturdy log houses. Thus today, we have the harbor settlement of St. James, through which passes Kings Highway. The highest sand dune is Mount Pisgah; the large inland lake at the south end is Lake Genesareth; the chief river is the Jordan; and the shallow baptismal lake at the north end is Font Lake.

This renaming of various places on the island added fuel to a fire which was already burning hot. A small group of Irish Catholic fishermen had established a settlement on what was known as Whiskey Point on the northeast side of the harbor, and they viewed with increasing animosity the build-up of the Mormon community.

Another source of friction was Strang's campaign against the fishermen's practice of trading whiskey for fish among the Indians on the island. Strang wrote in the newspaper he published that "Indian whiskey is made by putting two gallons of common whiskey, or unrectified spirits, into 30 gallons of water, adding enough red pepper to make it fiery, and tobacco enough to make it intoxicating. Its cost is not above five cents per gallon. Thousands of barrels have been sold every year, the prices generally being 50 cents a gallon by the cask, 25 cents a quart by the bottle, and 6 cents a drink."

The fishermen appealed to their friends at Mackinac for help. And in the summer of 1850 word spread at the Island and at Pine River (the present Charlevoix) about a Fourth of July celebration at Whiskey Point which was to culminate in driving the Mormons off the island. Over the water came canoes, skiffs, and Mackinaw boats. On Whiskey Point they unloaded food, drink, guns, and ammunition.

Strang countered by calling on his followers to form drill squads. And on the night of July 3rd, Mormon spies visited the carousing gentiles on Whiskey Point and threw some kegs of gunpowder into the lake. Next morning the Mormons pointed artillery across the harbor and saluted the Fourth with cannonballs which whistled toward Whiskey Point. The day wore on with no foray from Whiskey Point; the fishermen had lost their zeal for battle. They ate their beans and bacon, drank up their liquor, and boarded their boats with sunset finding them heading home to Mackinac and the mainland.

Several days later, however, the Mormons held a ceremony which further angered and astonished the gentiles. On July 8th beside the blue waters of Paradise Bay, Strang was crowned King of Beaver Island in fulfillment of another of his revelations. Clad in a crimson robe, the ruler marched to the platform with his twelve apostles, and there he was crowned with a tin circlet encrusted with glass stars. He read a decree imparted to him by revelation, ordaining the islands of the Great Lakes as the Kingdom of the Saints and delegating to the

King a portion of the lands to share among his people.

One of Strang's first royal pronouncements sanctioned poligamy among his people. He imparted a new revelation stating that God required the Saints to practice plural marriage. The King set an example by taking four wives into his household, but not many of his followers had prospered enough to enlarge their families. But the doctrine of poligamy quickly added to the notariety of the Mormons and to the outrage of their gentile neighbors.

During the early 1850s, Mormon numbers grew and colonies spread to Pine River, Grand Traverse Bay, and Drummond Island. On Beaver Island Strang's rule was undisputed. The Saints had driven out the earlier settlers who fled to neighboring islands. And on Mackinac, Mormon was an ugly word. Strang was elected to the Michigan legislature in 1852, and now the Mormons had threatening political power. In his first term of office, Strang accomplished the creation of Emmet County, comprising the Beaver Islands and a tract of neighboring mainland. Thus, he separated his kingdom from the authority of Mackinaw County. By 1855 King Strang was at the peak of his power. He was elected to a second term in the legislature. His kingdom embraced Beaver Island and all the outlying islands with a total population of 2600 Saints. His people were prosperous and for the most part loyal and happy. And the King's household had grown most royally. Each of his first two wives had bore him two children, and in the summer of 1855, he married two teenage cousins, each of whom shortly became pregnant.

But trouble with the gentiles was far from over. As a matter of fact, one of the worst outbreaks of violence had come in the summer of 1853, now known as the Battle of Pine River.

The trouble started when Strang tried to use his police

power to halt the sale of Indian whiskey to the Indians in the Pine River area on the mainland. On July 12th the Mormon sheriff of Emmet County, together with thirteen Beaver Islanders, put in at Pine River on what started out as a peaceful mission. They were issuing calls for jury duty in the Circuit Court at St. James on Beaver Island. As the sheriff and his men, all of them unarmed, started to leave and were launching their boats in the rather heavy surf of Lake Michigan, a number of Pine River settlers opened fire on them. About thirty men fired at close range from the beach, and another group fired down at the boats from a nearby bluff. Six Mormons were hit by gunfire, but they quickly rode out of range and headed for home, still a trip of 25 miles across open water.

But as they pulled away, they could see other boats being launched, the largest manned by twenty-four oarsmen. For ten miles the Mormons, with a little help from a light offshore breeze, were barely able to keep out of musket range of their pursuers. And half way to Beaver with the wind dying and nearly half of his men wounded, the sheriff was unable to maintain his margin of safety. Incredibly at this moment, a large vessel appeared on the horizon to the north, and the Mormons rowed to it with renewed vigor and were rescued. Strang called the survival of the Mormons "an extraordinary incident of the care of God for his creatures."

But Strang was to rue those words some three years later. Four of his henchmen, each of whom had suffered some indignities under Strang's harsh rule, plotted his assassination. They were led by Dr. Hezekiah McCulloch, a physician who had held some of the highest offices in the Strangist Church but who had fallen into disgrace because of a vice that Strang detested: drunkenness.

By some means, Dr. McCulloch was able to persuade

the battleship *Michigan* to visit St. James harbor. And on Monday, June 6, 1856, it put in at the dock in front of the store run by McCulloch, and the captain sent his pilot to summon Strang. As Strang strode down the dock, McCulloch and an ally caught up to him from the rear, and one of them shot Strang in the head at close range. As he fell, the prophet turned to face his assailants, and they shot him again in the face. As Strang rolled over, McCulloch discharged his horse pistol into the prophet's back. The two men then ran up the gangplank of the *Michigan* and asked for and received asylum.

The King was carried to a nearby house where the *Michigan*'s surgeon examined him and bandaged his wounds, but it was obvious that Strang was mortally wounded.

His two assailants, meanwhile, were returned to Mackinac Island by the *Michigan*, where they were quickly liberated and hailed as heroes by the towns-people. Beaver Island's threat to Mackinac finally had been destroyed.

On June 28th, Strang was taken aboard the steamer *Louisville* with four of his wives and their children and carried back to Voree, Wisconsin. There he died on July 9, 1856, almost exactly to the day six years after his coronation.

Meanwhile, gentile raiding parties from Mackinac harassed the islanders, and on July 5th a mob arrived to drive the Mormons from the island. Bands of half-drunk armed men roamed the island, herding Mormon farmers and their families at gunpoint to the dock at St. James and aboard waiting steamers. One boat took 490 to Chicago, another 300. The dispirited Mormons were so over-whelmed that none of them resisted to any extent. Within a span of a day or so an entire community of approximately 2600 men, women, and children was ruthlessly uprooted and cast out. One historian called it "The most disgraceful day in Michigan history."

Memories of the rule of King Strang still abound on Beaver Island. The Beaver Island Historical Society has preserved the old Mormon print shop where exhibits tell the story of the island kingdom. The society has also constructed a marine museum and preserved the Protar home.

At the print shop was published northern Michigan's first newspaper, with Strang as publisher. The marine museum is an authentic net shed built in 1906 and houses a growing collection of memorabilia from the days when St. James harbor was teeming with commercial activity.

The Protar home, built of hand hewn logs, stands in a rural setting, and it looks as it did when the noted "Doctor" Protar* occupied it from 1893 to his death in 1925.

The Irish returned to Beaver Island after the expulsion of the Mormons, and there they founded their own version of the Emerald Isle.

---

* See Appendix for more about "Doctor" Protar.

Mormon Print Shop *Beaver Island Historical Society photo*

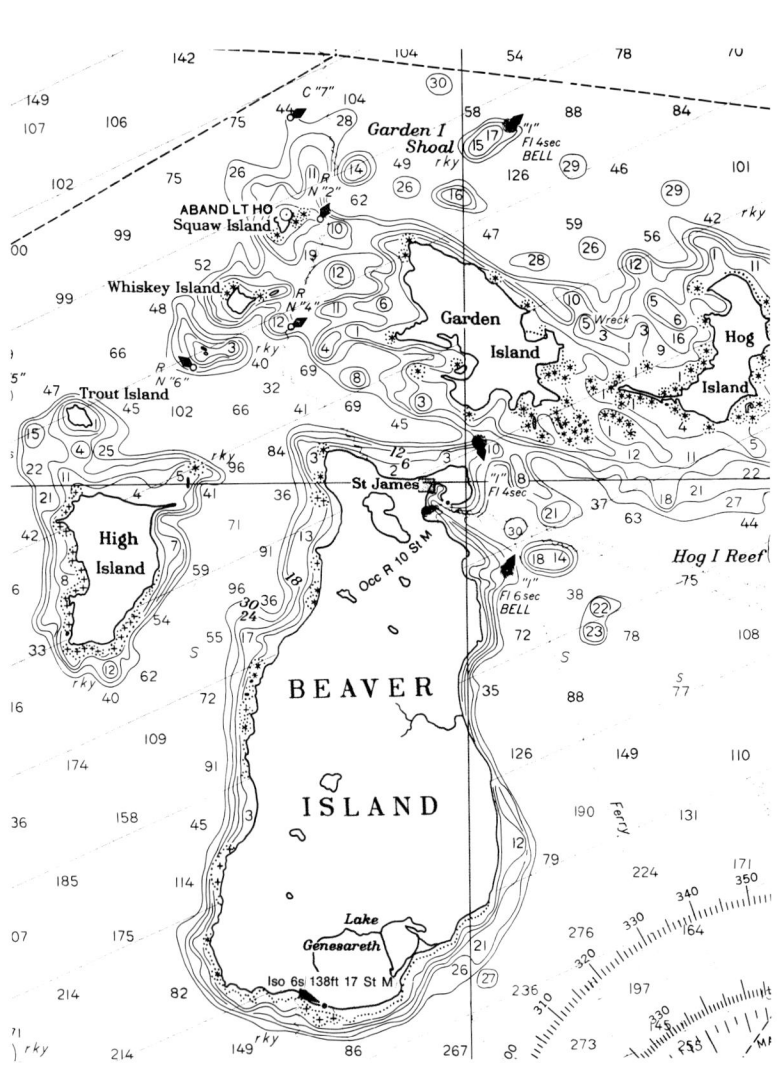

8

THE BEAVER ISLAND GROUP

No cruise of northern Lake Michigan is complete without a visit to fascinating Beaver Island and possible side trips to the other two once-inhabited islands in the area: High Island and Garden Island. Beaver lies approximately 35 miles northwest of Little Traverse Bay and some 40 miles southwest of the Straits of Mackinac.

Beaver Island was certainly visited by the earrliest of the French explorers of this area, including undoubtedly Jean Nicolet on his famous voyage in 1634. In 1672 the Beaver Islands appeared for the first time on a chart published in *Jesuit Relations*, based on the explorations of Marquette, Jolliet, and Allouez. When the island was named is uncertain, but why it was named Beaver is sure,

St. James — Beaver Island
Michigan Waterways Commission photo

Garden Island　　　　　　　　　　Robert T. McCoy photo

specifically because of the abundance of beaver which early trappers found there.

There were small white settlements off and on, but the first permanent community was established by James Strang when he moved his band of Mormons there in 1847. The Mormon settlement was broken up, and they left the island in 1856. At that point the Irish returned, and the island is now populated by fourth and fifth generation Americans of Irish descent; gentle, kindly, helpful, clever people who will welcome you to their island home. Irish jigs and reels are still danced in the St. James taverns on Saturday nights.

There is a fine protected harbor at the northeastern corner of Beaver Island; Beaver Harbor on the chart but Paradise Harbor as named by King Strang. And there are fine facilities at the docks at St. James.

Approach to St. James from the south or east is straight forward. Beware of the flashing green bell buoy off Stony Point to the south of the harbor entrance and then split the green spar marked C1 to the south and red nun #2 to the north. There is good water straight into the docks, but again leave red nun #4 to starboard. The harbor entrance is marked by a light on a 38-foot tower, occasionally red, but the light is not visible anywhere north of due east because of obstructing trees.

If approaching from the west around the north end of Beaver Island, be sure to pass close by the green lighted buoy in the channel between Garden and Beaver Islands and continue southeasterly so that you avoid shoal water off Sucker Point. Then round red nun #2 and proceed into the harbor as above.

The yacht dock is at the northwest end of the outer harbor just north of the ferry dock. Electricity, restrooms, showers, water, and pump-out are available. It may be possible to use the ferry dock's north edge, but be prepared to move if the ferry arrives.

For anchoring, the holding in the deep part of the outer harbor is not very good and is open to southeast blows. The better bet is the inner harbor, accessible through a marked channel. The inner harbor area behind the lighthouse point is the favored anchorage.

The city of St. James is the center of the bustling tourist trade on Beaver Island which is served by ferries twice a day from Charlevoix. There are a variety of stores available; hotels and motels, taxi service and car rentals, and medical services. One interesting activity is to rent a Moped and explore the island.

Most sailors head for the Shamrock Bar about two blocks up the street from the marina, where breakfast, lunch, and dinner are served along with all varieties of fermented beverages. Note the hundreds of personalized mugs hanging on the walls.

There are beautiful beaches all along the west shore of the island, and you can arrange a 30-mile automobile tour, seeing seven beautiful inland lakes. Perch fishing is good in the harbor, and black bass fishing is available in the inner lakes. A fishing license is required.

Most interesting, however, is a visit to several of the facilities developed by the Beaver Island Historical Society, notably the old Mormon print shop where memorabilia from the reign of King Strang are preserved, a marine museum with relics from a number of shipwrecks, and the home of "Doc" Protar, built of hand hewn logs, standing in a rural setting and looking as it did when the famous "doctor" occupied it from 1893 to the time of his death in 1925.

For yachtsmen who like to explore, a day's trip to Garden Island and/or High Island is well worthwhile.

High Island

Robert T. McCoy photo

POINT BETSIE LIGHT, LAKE MICHIGAN

The harbor at Garden Island should only be approached in fair weather and in daylight as there is a considerable amount of shoal water on either side of the entrance to the harbor. From St. James, the lighted green bell buoy north of Beaver Island should be passed close by and a course of 280 degrees magnetic maintained for three miles. Now proceed north directly toward the most westerly edge of Garden Island which will bear about 15 degrees. Proceed about one and one-half miles until the center of Garden Island harbor bears 87 degrees. From here take a course for the center of Garden Island Bay into the harbor. The bad spots to watch for are the 8-foot spot to the west of this course, the 5-foot spots to the north of this course, and the rock-awash reef on the south side of the course. Obviously, proceed slowly and with caution.

There are good anchorages almost up to shore in the land-locked northwest corner of the harbor and another excellent anchorage behind the island in the southeast corner of the harbor. To get behind this island, round its north side and then go south.

Once you have dinghied ashore there are roads and trails leading to many interesting spots for exploration.

High Island to the west had a somewhat similar history to that of Beaver. It was settled in 1912 by a group from the House of David at Benton Harbor, Michigan and was used as a penal colony by this religious sect and was known as the "Siberia of Michigan." In the course of its existence, the colony grew to over 100 families, but King Ben* was arrested in 1928 and jailed and about this time the inhabitants deserted, leaving everything behind them. Some of the remains of this colony are still to be seen, particularly the octagon-shaped harem which was King

---

* See appendix for more about King Ben.

Ben's home when he was living on the island. The main road fronting the harbor leads west to high hills along the western shore of the island and down through a narrow trail to a very fine beach. The sailor with mountain climbing ability will be well rewarded for his climb in reaching the top of the several 200- to 250-foot elevations on this western side of the island where on a clear day one can have a sweeping view of 20-30 miles of the surrounding territory.

There is a deep harbor on the northeast corner of the island which is really only a minor indentation in the shore. The harbor is exposed to easterly winds and therefore is usually visited only for day trips out of St. James. There are no danger points approaching this harbor except for the long point and two very small islands at the northeast corner. The islands are sandy, low, and hard to see but are marked with a red spar.

There is up to 30 feet of water close to shore in the northwest corner of the harbor. The ruins of an old dock are under water close into shore as indicated on the chart. There is good holding, and the water is so clear that on a still day bottoms up to 30 feet may be seen.

As I remarked earlier, a visit to the Beaver Island group is a must, and sailors who wish to explore the outer islands could well plan to spend several days here.

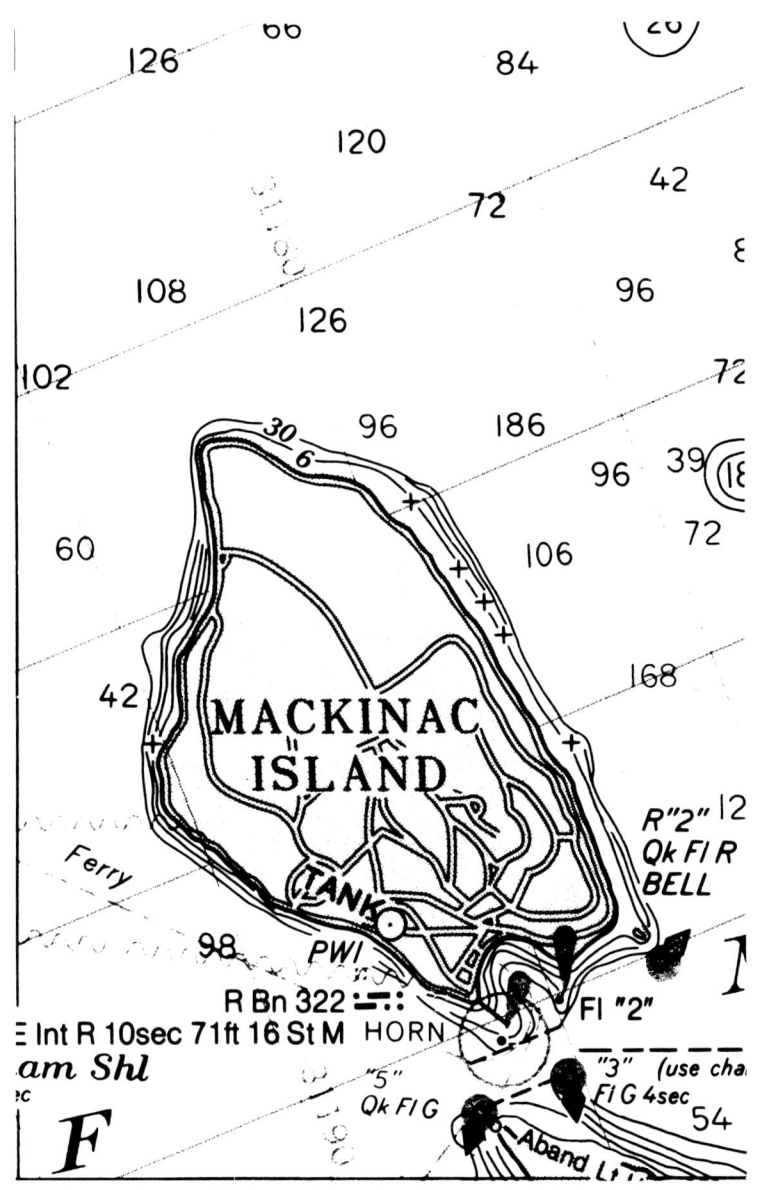

9

THE ISLAND

The first time you sail a boat under the bridge crossing the Straits of Mackinac it will be one of your greatest thrills asea, and it is not much less of a thrill in subsequent passages. The beautiful span is visible in good weather as soon as you have completed the Grays Reef passage and made your turn east to enter the Straits. Sailors with local knowledge cut the corner after navigating the passage, but good sense dictates continuing north past bell buoy #3 before heading east.

Once past the bridge, buoys will mark Majors Shoal to starboard and Graham Shoals to port. Then head straight into the channel between Round Island to starboard and Mackinac Island to port. The marina is just past the southernmost point of the Island.

There are a large number of slips in the public marina on the Island, but they are usually crowded. The dockmasters do a fine job, however, of accommodating visiting

Mackinac Island *Michigan Waterways Commission photo*

Mackinaw City   *Michigan Waterways Commission photo*

yachtsmen. Upon entering the harbor contact the dockmaster by radio, and he will respond, usually by asking the skipper to go into a holding pattern to the east of the marina. There will generally be other boats circling in that area and newcomers pick a spot in line. When space is available, the dockmaster will call for your boat, and if there isn't a slip immediately available, he will often arrange for you to tie up stern-to at the outer end of of a finger pier.

Full facilities are available: gasoline and diesel fuel, electricity, water, pump-out, and restrooms. Showers are available across the road at the rear of the Mackinac Yacht Club building where an attendant will charge you a nominal fee.

Once docked and settled in you are ready to experience the fascination of a visit to this historic island. Motor vehicles are prohibited, and transportation is by foot, bicycle or horse.

The best way to get an overall view of the Island is to take one of the horse and buggy rides on a sightseeing tour. If you are familiar with horses, you can also rent you own horse and carriage from a livery stable, and horses are also available for riding around the Island. Another good way to tour the Island is by bicycle, and they are readily available for rent.

The Island has been a state park for nigh unto a hundred years now, and the state has done a magnificent job of restoring the fort buildings. They are manned by guides in the uniforms of the period when the fort was occupied, interpreting life there in the 19th century. They fire their muskets and the fort's cannons. Reveille is sounded every morning when the Stars and Stripes are run up the flagpole, and the sound of taps coming down the hillside in the evening will make the spine tingle. There are guided tours of the fort, and exhibits and dioramas tell the colorful history of the fortifications. A tea room at the fort serves soups, salads, and sandwiches.

There are a variety of unique shops and a number of fine restaurants along the main street fronting the harbor. The tourists who come to the Island by ferry from St. Ignace or Mackinaw City are known as "fudgies" since most of them will return home with a box of the famous fudge made in the shops on the island. Among the restaurants, the Pink Panther bar and dining room in the Chippewa Hotel is a favorite with sailors. For family dining, Little Bob's is recommended; also Ty's. There is a good Mexican restaurant, Little Mexico, up the street. Horn's Gaslight Bar also specializes in Mexican food, and the dining room in the Murray Hotel has long been popular. A visit to the Grand Hotel is a must, including a relaxing pause for a drink on the huge veranda overlooking the harbor, followed by dinner in the hotel dining room.

If you have children aboard, take them to the T-shirt shop to have their own memento of the Island made. There are also some very nice gift shops on the back street just a block in from the harbor, particularly some good cheese shops.

After a good dinner ashore or on board and after the last of the tourists have been ferried back to the mainland, yachtsmen will really appreciate the quiet and beauty of the Island.

There are two good harbor facilities on the mainland, both north and south of the Straits.

At Mackinaw City on the south side, the marina has 4 to 12 feet of water and provides gas, pump-out, water, electricity, and ice. The marina is one block from the main shopping center where all types of supplies are available. There is airline limo service to Pellston airport if you are

Island's Main Street *Michigan Travel Bureau photo*

The Grand Hotel *Michigan Travel Bureau photo*

intending to change crews at this point. The Shepler Marine Service is located just south of the marina and has a 12-ton capacity travel-lift, a ship's store, complete Canadian and U.S. charts, and full repair services. Shepler monitors channel 16.

Another good place to change crews is on the north side of the Straits at St. Ignace, which is on the main highway from the south. The public dock is located just south of the ferry dock and is marked with a flashing red light on a 10-foot mast. Transient facilities are usually available here, and the dock has gasoline, water, electricity, and fine restroom and shower facilities; also pump-out. The dock attendant monitors channel 16. The main street of St. Ignace is just up from the marina, and all types of supplies are immediately available here. Several blocks up the street is The Galley, the only restaurant I know of that serves whitefish livers on its regular menu, and the two-block walk will prove well worth it when you sip a fine dry martini, followed with a luncheon of braised livers and a nice dry white wine.

All in all, a visit to the Mackinac area is well worth several days on your cruise, and there are a number of further options for exploratory visits in the area which we will outline in the next chapter.

St. Ignace *Michigan Waterways Commission photo*

SUMMER SAIL II 109

Tour The Island By Carriage   *Michigan Travel Bureau photo*

Fort From The Marina *Michigan Travel Bureau photo*

The Bridge As Seen From The Fort
Michigan Travel Bureau photo

Fort Guns Fire *Fitzgerald photo*

M & L S R R
Manistique
River
Indian River
MANISTIQUE
R MAST
(WTIQ)
1490 kHz
TANK
R RELAY MASTS
AERO
Dutch Johns Point
Gull
AN
E
rky
30
Iso R 6s 50ft 12 St M
HORN
47800
47820
6
12
18
24
5
42
28
15
53
43
46
29
19
16
18
35
27
52
34
49
61
22
Naubinway
Biddle Point
Davenport
Naubinway I Lt
Fl 4sec 32ft 6 St M
Naubinway
Reef
Pelkie Reef
ry Shoal
R
N "2"
Millecoquins Reefs
C "1"
rky
15
36
11
43
14
20
28
33
53
4
47
38
17
22
16
26
39
40
49
60
69
51
38
6
25
54
21
66
68
10
7
60
68

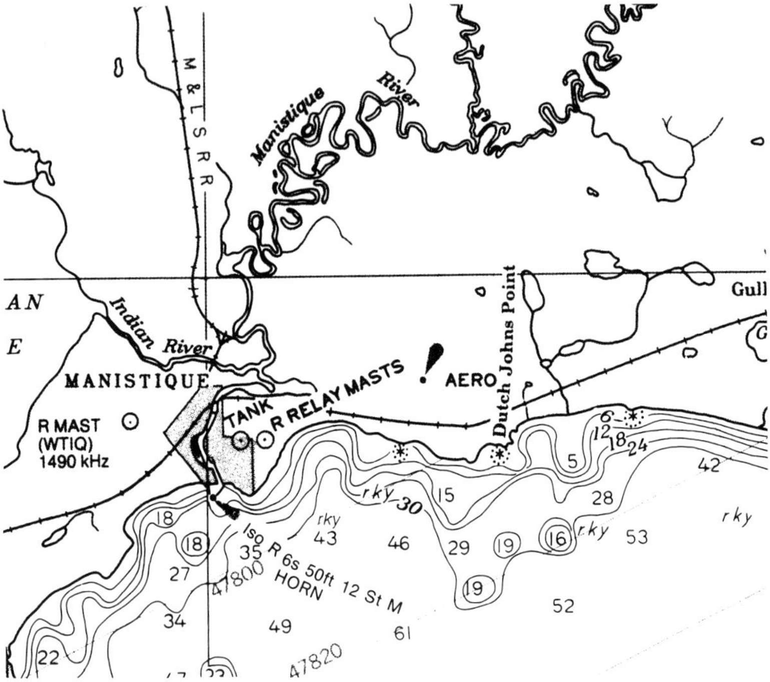

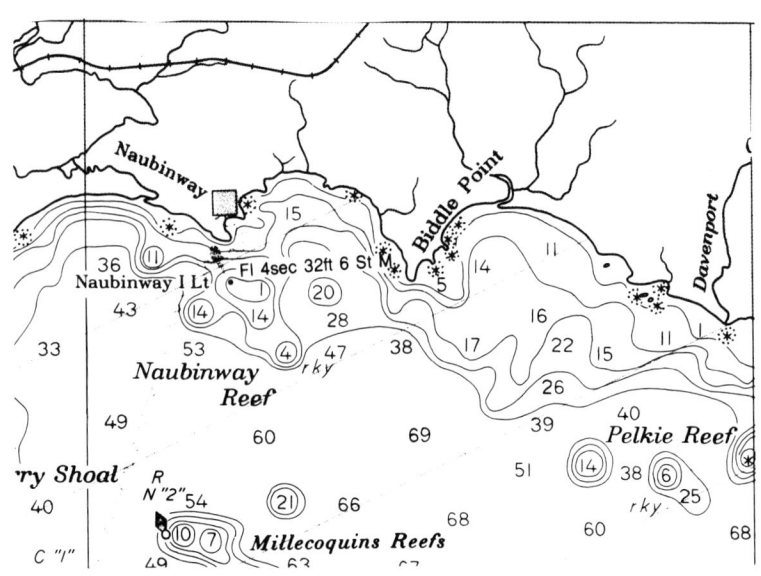

10

CRUISING WEST TO MANISTIQUE

Mackinac Island has long been considered the goal of many cruises, but it can also be the base of operations for a further cruise or even a series of cruises in almost any direction.

There are many fine harbors within roughly 55 miles east or west of the Island. Here are the entrances to Lake Superior, the passage from Lake Michigan into Lake Huron, and the entrance to the North Channel and Georgian Bay. The north end of Lake Michigan is relatively well protected water for some 50 miles west of the Straits, with the series of islands forming Grays Reef and then the Beaver Island group sheltering the area from the south.

This is one of the routes sailors might opt to take if they are heading for the Garden Peninsula of Upper Michigan

Manistique *Michigan Waterways Commission photo*

Naubinway *Michigan Travel Bureau photo*

and the northern areas of Green Bay.

There are three harbors located along the north shore of the lake, starting with Naubinway, some 40 miles west of the Straits. This is a small fishing and resort village, formerly a boomtown in the lumbering era. It now serves as the gateway to a 35,000 acre wilderness paradise called the Hiawatha Sportsmens Club. A short distance north of the harbor are miles of sand trails through pine forests and aspen groves. It is a private club, but visiting yachtsmen are welcome. It is a paradise for bird watchers.

There is a new marina with 14 slips in the harbor. Naubinway Island is marked by a flashing white light on a white skeleton tower, visible for six miles. From the island swing to starboard to clear Millecoquin's Point and then round up to the west of the dock. Most facilities are available at the dock: gasoline, electricity, water plus showers and restrooms. Diesel is available by truck delivery, and ice, groceries, bakery, and so forth are readily available in town. Naubinway is an out of the way port and sees few transient boats, but the residents are most friendly and will drive you around town if you so desire.

There is a harbor which can be used for refuge between Naubinway and Manistique at Port Inland, but Michigan has not developed a public facility here yet and there is little information available on this harbor. Not true, however, of Manistique, which sits at the northwest corner of Lake Michigan and is the gateway to the Garden Peninsula and then Green Bay.

The harbor offers excellent protection under all weather conditions, and good docking facilities and anchorage areas are available. Yachts approaching Manistique from the east should note and avoid the rocky shoal water off Farnsworth Point and a shoal lying off the point just east of the harbor entrance. When approaching from the southwest, note and leave to port Wiggins Point Shoal 10 miles south of Manistique, marked by a red lighted bell buoy.

The harbor is entered on course 29 degrees true between lights on the ends of converging breakwaters. A channel 18 feet deep extends from the outer breakwater up to 400 feet inside the mouth of the Manistique River. There is a flashing white light on the breakwater to port; flashing red on the breakwater to starboard; and then a flashing green light on the end of the west pierhead, which should be left to port. The yacht basin is just inside the mouth of the river on the starboard side.

Gasoline, electricity, and restrooms with showers are available. The main business district of Manistique is two blocks from the harbor, and transportation to shopping areas and restaurants is available. Marine repair service is available at all times.

The city of Manistique offers the visitor big town facilities with small town friendliness. There are a wide variety of shopping facilities, a modern hospital, and newly remodeled airport capable of handling small business jets. There is a beautiful sand beach just east of the breakwater.

The marina at Manistique has gained a reputation as one of the finest on the Great Lakes, and while it is not very well known, it is an interesting place for the adventurous sailor to visit. It is 40 miles from Manistique to Beaver Island southeast, and about the same distance to the entrance of Green Bay.

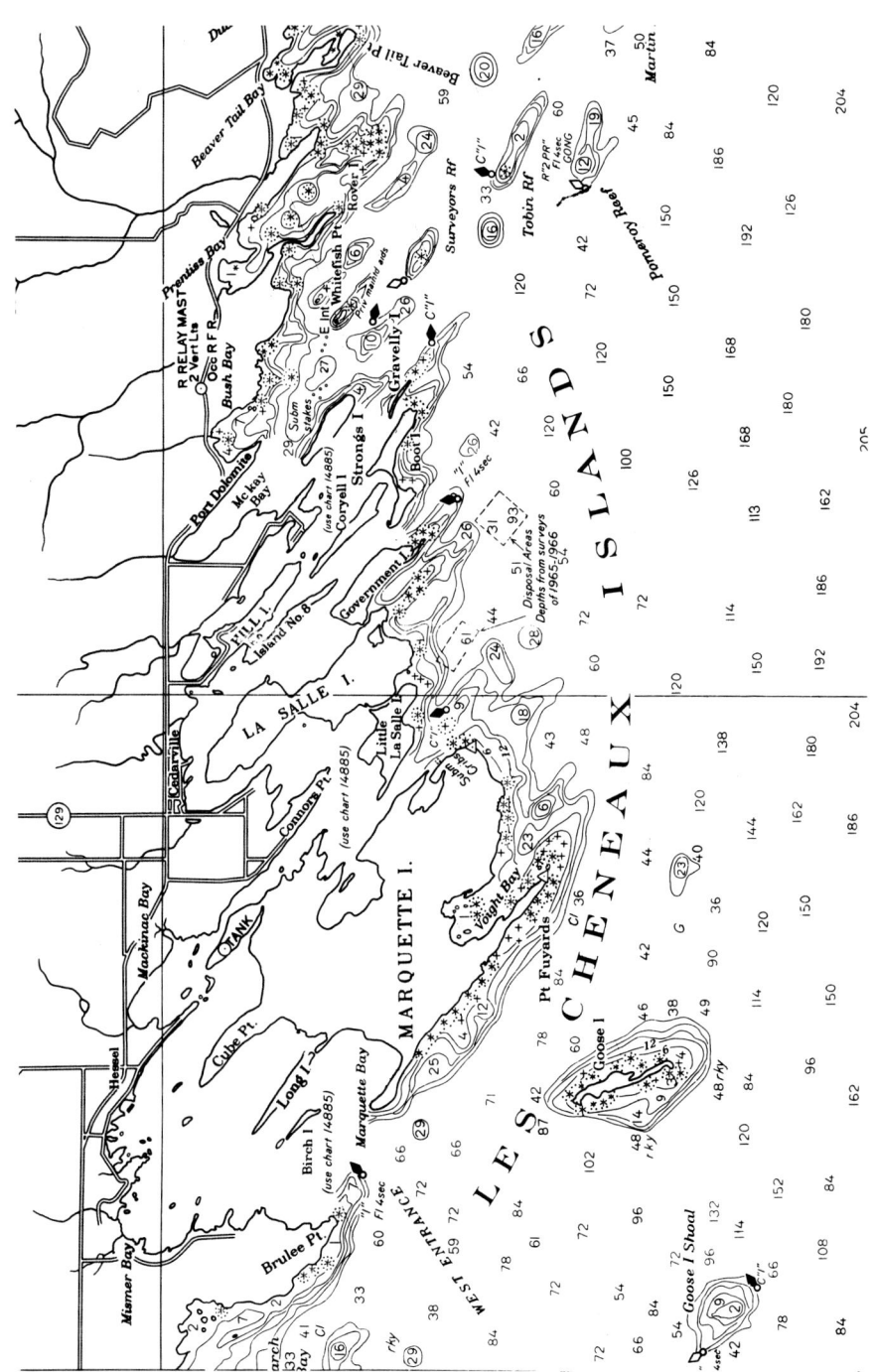

11

LES CHENEAUX ISLANDS

An easy sail northeast of Mackinac will bring you to a delightful cluster of islands and headlands popularly known as "The Snows." This is a corruption of their proper name, Les Cheneaux Islands, the English translation of which is "The Channels." And channels there are, many of them very adequately marked by the Channel Island Association. There are two ports within the complex: Hessel on the west and Cedarville to the east.

The west entrance to the islands is about 12 miles from Mackinac between Brulle Point and Marquette Island.

Charts #14880 and #14885 will give you detailed information on the channels in the islands. For channel marking purposes, Cedarville is considered the home port, so the red buoys are to starboard approaching Cedarville.

Hessel *Michigan Waterways Commission photo*

SOUTH MANITOU LIGHT, LAKE MICHIGAN

Approaching from the west the course is 42 degrees true from Mission Point's lighted bell buoy R2 at Mackinac Island. The west entrance is marked with Brulle Point lighted buoy B1. And from there you will pick up buoys #2, #3, and #4 into Hessel Bay. The Michigan state yacht basin at Hessel has 8 to 9 feet of water along the dock on the inner side. It features a boat launching ramp, showers, restrooms, and electricity.

The best entrance approaching from the east is at Government Island. There is a least depth of 13 feet (LWD) to the head of Government Bay and then 7 feet through the buoyed channel to Cedarville. Approaching from the east, when Martin Reef light bears 0 degrees at a distance of one and one-half miles, steer 301 degrees true to clear Pomeroy Reef buoy R2 and continue to Penny Island buoy B1. Here you will pick up the small boat course shown on chart #14885. Exercise special care in the narrow passages of the islands, as landowners have experienced considerable damage from heavy wakes. Yachtsmen are requested to hold their speed to a point where the transom is not pulling. Bow waves are not nearly as damaging to properties as transom pull.

There is no public marina at Cedarville, but several of the private docks will accommodate a limited number of transient boats.

Groceries, ice, gasoline, and water are available at either Hessel or Cedarville, and there are several restaurants, but none of them are outstanding. The only laundromat is at Cedarville.

A visit to the Cheneaux Islands is more for their beauty than for the facilities available in the harbors. There are, incidentally, many good places for anchoring, particularly in Marquette Bay, the bay lying southwest of Cube Point, Muscallonge Bay, Government Bay, and Scammons

Harbor. All have good water, good protection, and they lie along the charted course.

It is beautiful just sailing or motoring through the channels of the islands and observing the many fine summer homes built here by people generally from the Detroit area who discovered the Cheneaux Islands a number of years ago. They have become even more popular since the building of the bridge across the Straits.

Tied up at the docks of the cottages on the islands, you will note many beautiful runabouts, many of which are carefully maintained antiques. As a matter of fact, an annual antique boat show is held in the islands the first Saturday in August, and Chris-Craft buffs make an annual pilgrimage here.

The Cheneaux are a delightful stopping off place when cruising to and from the North Channel. It's about another 20 miles to DeTour Passage, the entrance to the North Channel leading east to Georgian Bay; and about the same distance to the St. Mary's River leading north and west through Sault Ste. Marie into Lake Superior. But these are subjects for entire books in themselves, which we may get around to writing in another year or so. For now, let's return to the Mackinac area and shoot the choke, so to speak.

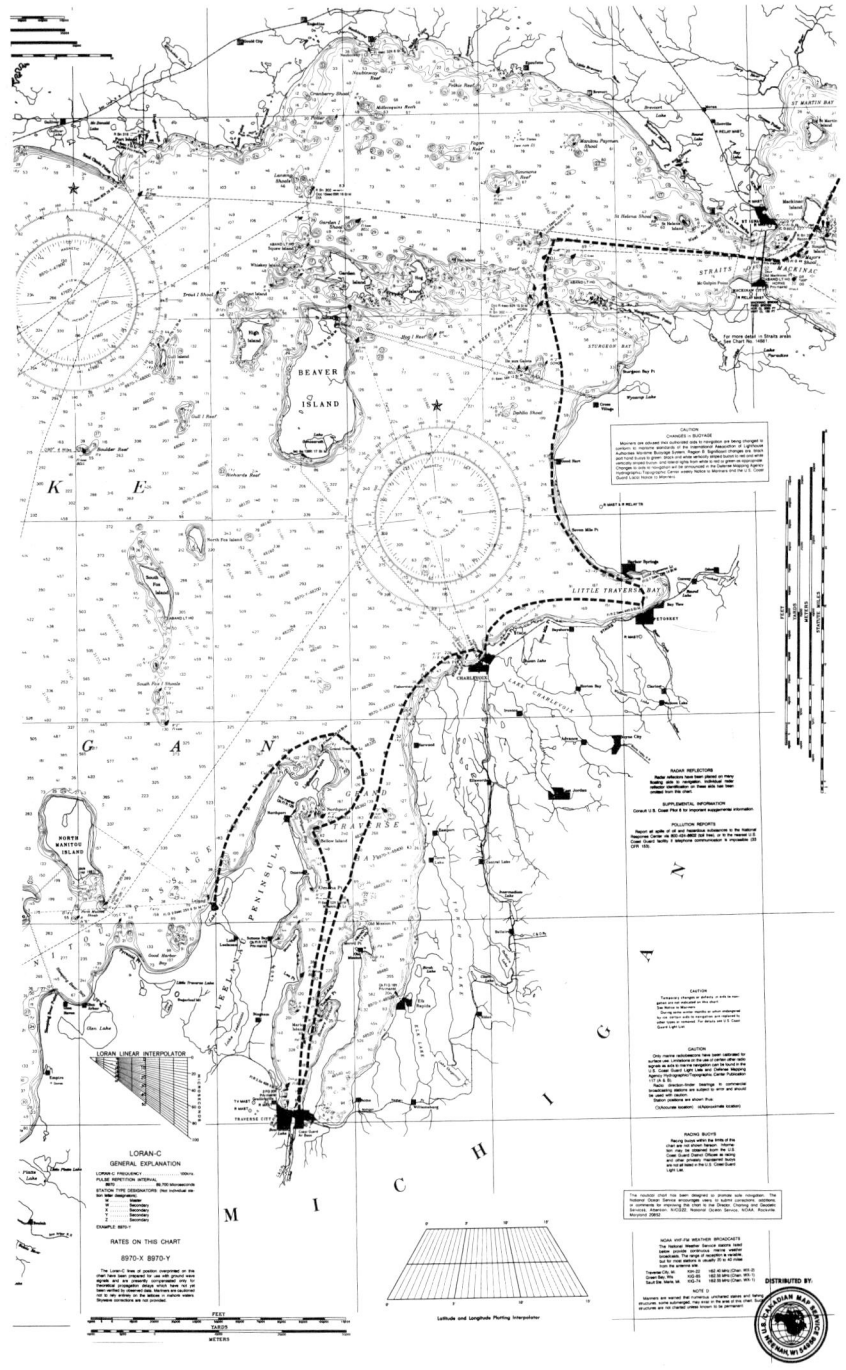

12

SUGGESTED TWO WEEK CRUISE

As I did in *Summer Sail: Cruising the Historic Waters of Green Bay,* I would like to suggest an itinerary for a two week cruise of northern Lake Michigan.

Let's begin at Leland, which most sailors from the southern and western areas of Lake Michigan consider to be the starting point for a cruise of these waters. And let's plan to pick up some fresh whitefish at the market near the dock for a quiet dinner at the Leland marina that night. May be you will be lucky and be able to buy some whitefish livers for your cocktail hour.

We can take some time our second morning to supply up at Leland since the shopping is so convenient. In the afternoon, we will cross the 16-mile Manitou Channel over to South Manitou Island, arriving there in time to secure a good anchorage and dinghy ashore for a walk around the southern end of the island, marvelling at the world record white cedar trees in the Valley of the Giants and winding up sitting atop a high sand dune bluff on the west shore of the island as the sun sets over Lake Michigan. The sunsets from this area along the eastern shore of Lake Michigan you will remember for many years to come.

On our third day out, we will sail approximately 30 miles northeast to Charlevoix, and this should get us in there by early afternoon, where we hopefully can get a slip at the public marina in Round Lake or if not in some of the other private facilities in either Round Lake or Lake Charlevoix. This would probably be a good evening to take the first mate ashore for a fine dinner at one of the good supper clubs in Charlevoix. And she will want to spend part of the next day shopping the very unique shops in this resort village.

We want to get her back on board by early afternoon so that we can enjoy a sail on beautiful Lake Charlevoix whose waters are crystal clear. Given the prevailing south to southwest winds you can generally expect to have a very nice reaching sail both ways on Lake Charlevoix, possibly stopping for the evening at Boyne City.

We are going to want to make the 30-odd miles to St. James Harbor on Beaver Island on our fifth day out, but it would be perfectly all right if we arrived there in late afternoon so that we can spend the next day exploring either Beaver Island or one of the adjoining islands: Garden or High or both.

Plan for sure to have at least a cocktail at the Shamrock Bar, but you may also want to stay for supper.

It is an easy run now of a little over 40 miles through the Grays Reef Passage to Mackinac Island so that we should arrive there by mid-afternoon on our seventh day. We will spend the eighth and ninth days here on the Island since there is much to see and enjoy. Be sure that you take a tour of historic Fort Mackinac and stay long enough to witness the mounting of the guard. Plan also to have at least cocktails at the Grand Hotel one of these evenings and have dinner there or in one of the good restaurants along the harbor.

On the tenth day, let's make an expedition to Les Cheneaux Islands which are only 12 to 15 miles away, depending upon which harbor you choose: Hessel or Cedarville. It is relatively easy to visit them both and that would give you a good tour through the channels of the islands, the channels from which they acquire their name. There is not much to hold us here for the evening, however, so let's return to St. Ignace and spend the night at the very nice harbor facility there.

We will take a walk several blocks up the main thoroughfare of St. Ignace and treat ourselves to whitefish livers at The Galley restaurant, if we haven't been able to try them at one of the fish markets along the way.

We will have a 50-mile sail on our eleventh day to Little Traverse Bay where I suggest we put up the first night at Harbor Springs, taking a walking tour of that very delightful resort community. On the twelfth day, I suggest crossing the bay to Petoskey, where a visit to the gaslight district in the village is well worthwhile, particularly in the evening.

We are going to limit our visit to Grand Traverse Bay to the harbor at Northport in this two week's cruise, with the idea that if you have more time at your disposal you can then head from there down to Traverse City or take advantage of some of the very nice secluded anchorages along both arms of Grand Traverse Bay.

Northport is a delightful little community in its own right, however, and will provide us with an easy cruise back to Leland to finish up our two weeks.

I think you will agree with me that two weeks is barely enough to enjoy these beautiful waters and these delightful resort communities. But at another time and place, I may suggest passing up some of these harbors to shoot on up to the Straits of Mackinac and accompany me in another book to the North Channel of Lake Huron and Georgian Bay.

Veranda Of The Grand Hotel *Fitzgerald photo*

ROUND ISLAND LIGHT, STRAITS OF MACKINAC

APPENDIX

F. Protar   *Beaver Island Historical Society photo*

F. PROTAR

On his tombstone is the name FEODORA PROTAR, but was that really the name of this mysterious man of Beaver Island?

Much conjecture has been made about "Doctor" Protar concerning his life before he made Beaver Island his home permanently in 1893. One thing is certain: he was not a licensed physician but he did practice medicine in his own limited way; thus, the title of doctor given to him by his patients and neighbors on Beaver Island.

Antje Price wrote what is probably the most definitive piece on "Doctor" Protar in *The Journal of Beaver Island History — Volume One — 1976* (published by the Beaver Island Historical Society). Price is to be commended for exemplary research into the life of this remarkable man and for not falling prey to the great temptation to sensationalize and offer up even more conjecture.

The facts concerning Protar's life before coming to

Beaver Island are somewhat scanty. Known for certain are:

Protar is an anagram for PARROT, his true family name. He was of German ancestry. He came to America in the 1860s as an actor. He lived in Rock Island, Illinois for a number of years and owned and operated a newspaper there. He was married in 1867 but became a widower in 1872 when his wife Louise passed away. He purchased the Connelly farm in April 1893, moved in, and as far as is known, never left the island again.

Exactly how Protar became a "doctor" is uncertain. He did not call himself a physcian and would not tolerate anyone addressing him by that title. He acted more as a pharmacist, dispensing medicines along with advice on how to treat the ailment. Like modern medical practitioners, he did not make house calls; his "patients" came to him. The islanders respected this recluse, then honored him after his passing in 1925 by erecting a significant tombstone to his memory over his grave which is on the property he owned.

Contributing to the mystery of Protar is his relationship with Dr. Carl Bernhardi. They were friends; that is certain. What else? Uncertain. Adding to the strangeness of their friendship is that both men died on the same day, Protar passing away before Bernhardi — he died in a Chicago hospital — by a mere matter of hours.

The concluding paragraph of Price's piece best describes the man Beaver Islanders knew as "Doctor" Protar:

"An essential part of Protar's creed was to be a humble, secret giver. But his gift shines through the gruffness and reticence with which he armed himself against the world and illuminates his existence. Though a conscientious man who had the courage to live his principles to the exclusion of the external world, he would most vehemently have insisted that he was too imperfect to be called a saint, as he would not tolerate being called 'doctor,' or being exalted in any way. The islanders, who could never know him well, accepted him for what he was to them, but the quality of their memory, in simple gratitude and admiration as a friend, shows that they did understand and value the man he was trying to be."

Protar's home and tomb remain as memorials to him and his way of life. The house stand across from the Centennial Farm of his good neighbors, the Bonners, and is registered as a national historic site. The Beaver Island Historical Society maintains the property which is open to the public.

"KING BEN"

When most people hear "House of David", they are inclined to picture bearded baseball players. But not so in Benton Harbor, Michigan or around the Beaver Island Group. The name has an entirely different connotation in said parts.

"King Ben" was Benjamin Purnell, a colorful character with a flaming red beard and shoulder-length hair, who claimed to be the "Seventh Messenger" referred to in the Book of Revelations in the Holy Bible. He founded the House of David in Benton Harbor around the turn of the century. In 1912, land on High Island was purchased by the sect, and a colony was begun there.

Like almost all minor religious groups, the House of David is often referred to as a cult because of some out of the ordinary belief and/or because its members might live in a communal style, sharing everything from work to rewards and, as those not necessarily in the know would add, beds. As an example of this, an octagonal building on High Island where the sect's young women were housed was called the "Harem" by outsiders, whereas the "Israelites" referred to it as the "House of Virgins" because girls were kept there under guard until they reached marrying age. This was rather contradictory in the House of David because marriage was an unfulfilled institution for its membership.

The settlement on High Island was also said to be a penal colony for wayward members of the sect, but Grant Hart and Phil Gregg in their piece on the House of David in *The Journal of Beaver Island History — Volume One — 1976* make no references to this being so. Again, rumor to be taken with a grain of salt.

The facts are, according to Hart and Gregg, the Israelites of High Island were a hardy, industrious, peaceful people, well-liked by their neighbors on Beaver Island. They made no attempts at politics or at domination of their neighbors as the Mormons of the previous century did. Instead they grew their vegetables, cut their timber, and minded their own business.

"King Ben" rarely visited High Island, spending most of his time at Benton Harbor, the home of the sect. He was dubbed king by the newspapers, the "yellow press" of his time, which sought more to sensationalize than to report the news in order to entice readership and influence. It is true that Purnell behaved despotically and served his own comfort ahead of others. But most of the other tales concerning him and his followers were farfetched prattlings by misinformed and/or ignorant tongue-waggers with nothing better to do than attack that which they did not know and understand and thus fear.

"King Ben" attracted converts to the House of David by informing them they were "Israelites" and thus were

God's "chosen people" and would live until all else passed away and the Kingdom of God was established on earth. When one of his flock unceremoniously did pass into the next life, it was said on Beaver Island that "his faith had lapsed." The deceased was then excommunicated and buried elsewhere.

Hart and Gregg do not tell whether this was done to Purnell when he died in December 1927, leaving his flock to tend for itself. They do relate how a legal battle for control of the sect's assets ensued between Purnell's widow, "Queen Mary", and a Judge Dewhirst. A settlement was reached three years later, and Dewhirst was given control of the High Island colony. The Israelites there were not consulted about their wishes, and their wish was to remain faithful to "Queen Mary".

That fall Dewhirst sent one Billy Wright to supervise the evacuation of Mary's loyalists, also charging him with the duty of doing an inventory of his newly acquired assets. But with the colder months rapidly coming on, Wright held off taking full action until the following year.

During the winter, some of the more enterprising Beaver Islanders "traded" some of their rather mangy farm animals for those on High Island which were far superior in quality. This was done without the knowledge of Wright, and when he returned to the island in spring and saw the feeble stock, he could do little but stroke his beard and mumble something about it having been a hard winter.

Little remains of the House of David settlement, but any exploration of High Island is more worthwhile with a knowledge of its history.

DR. BEAUMONT AND THE MAN WITH THE LID ON HIS STOMACH

A fascinating incident in the history of Mackinac Island is depicted at the fort hospital, the story of "the man with the lid on his stomach."

It began in 1820 when a young French *voyageur*, Alexis St. Martin, accidentally shot himself in the stomach while examining a shotgun in the fur company store. The fort surgeon, Dr. William Beaumont, was summoned, and he attended the young man as he lay on a cot in the rear of the store. "The whole mass of materials from the musket together with pieces of clothing and pieces of fractured ribs were driven into the chest cavity," the doctor was to write later. He gave him less than 36 hours to live.

But Dr. Beaumont had not counted on the toughness of

the French *voyageur*. When he returned a few hours later he found St. Martin recovering from the shock, so he cleaned and dressed the wound and had St. Martin moved to the fort hospital.

By the next day St. Martin was alert and hungry. The patient was fed under the watchful eye of the physician, and observing that food was passing out through the wound, Dr. Beaumont applied firm dressings, walling in the stomach. After the fourth week, Dr. Beaumont wrote: "The appetite became good, digestion regular."

The rest of the story became medical history. The inner abrasions from the wound began to heal, but the flesh at the surface would not close, despite the doctor's efforts to excite adhesions. A compress held in the contents of the stomach. Eventually a fold of flesh grew like a flap to cover the stomach opening.

Realizing that he had a unique, living laboratory for medical experimentation, Dr. Beaumont took St. Martin into his household, nursed him, fed him, clothed him, lodged him, all on the condition that St. Martin would submit to the doctor's experimentation.

Through the flap in St. Martin's stomach, Beaumont was able to view firsthand the stomach's digestive processes and over the next few years, he reported 238 detailed observations of the chemical action of the stomach in digesting a great variety of foods which he fed his patient.

The pair were separated when Dr. Beaumont was transferred to Fort Niagara and then Fort Howard in Green Bay (where, incidentally, the Beaumont Hotel is named for him). But they were united again at Fort Crawford at Prairie du Chien, and there the experiments resumed with "the man with the lid on his stomach," as St. Martin became known.

CREDITS

Aerial photos by Robert T. McCoy of Wauwatosa, Wisconsin, and by the Michigan Waterways Commission.

Additional photos and information from the Michigan Travel Bureau.

Cover art by Keith Ward of Milwaukee, and the paintings of the lighthouses by Chuck Forman of Rapid City, Michigan.

And special warm thanks to my sailing buddies, Rockne and Patti Fitzgerald. Patti transcribed all my rambling dictation; Rocky critiqued it and provided pictures out of his personal files.

BIBLIOGRAPHY

Port Pilot and Log Book — Great Lakes Cruising Club

Michigan Harbors Guide — Michigan Waterways Commission

West Michigan Vacation Guide — West Michigan Tourist Association

The Guide for Northwestern Michigan — Petoskey News-Review

Michigan's Upper Peninsula — Upper Peninsula Travel and Recreation Association

Three Flags at the Straits — Walter Havighurst

100 Years in Leelanau — Edmund G. Littell

King Strang — Robert P. Weeks

The Ottawan — J. C. Wright

Petoskey in Ye Olden Days — Floy Irene Graham

The Journal of Beaver Island History, Volume One, 1976
 — Beaver Island Historical Society

INDEX

A
Allouez - 91
American Fur Company - 18, 19
Ann Arbor, Michigan - 79
Appalachia - 25
Astor, John Jacob - 19
Atlantic Ocean - 23, 82

B
Bay View - 71
Bay View Inn - 71
Bear River - 69
Beaumont, Dr. William - 141, 142
Beaumont Hotel - 142
Beaver Harbor - 94
Beaver Island - 62, 66, 79, 83, 84, 85, 86, 87, 88, 91, 92, 94, 95, 98, 119, 128, 135, 139, 140

Beaver Island Group - 11, 79, 85, 91, 99, 115, 138
Beaver Island Historical Society - 88, 95, 135, 137
Bellow Island - 53, 49, 94
Benton Harbor - 98, 138, 139, 140
Bernhardi, Carl - 136
Between The Covers Bookstore - 74
Bluebird (restaurant) - 37
Bowers Harbor - 48, 53
Bowers Harbor Inn - 45
Boyne City - 63, 64, 128
Brulle Point - 121
Buffalo, New York - 82
Burlington, Wisconsin - 80, 81
Burt Lake - 75

C

Canada - 15
Candlelight (restaurant) - 71
Carlson's Fisheries - 37
Carp Lake - 36
Carp River - 37
Carthage, Illinois - 81
Cat Head Point - 41
Cedarville - 121, 124, 129
Channel Island Association - 121
Charlevoix - 53, 55, 56, 57, 58, 59, 61, 62, 63, 66, 67, 95, 128
Charlevoix, Pierre du - 59
Cheboygan River - 75
Chicago -19, 20, 44, 59, 87, 136
Chicago-to-Mackinac Race - 20, 75
Chippewa Hotel - 105
Chippewa Indians (*see Ojibway Indians*)
Church of Jesus Christ of Latter-Day Saints - 80, 82

Civil War - 20
Colonial Inn - 74
Country Lantern (restaurant) - 71
Crooked Lake - 75, 76
Cube Point - 124

D

Detour Passage - 125
Detroit - 20, 125
Detroit *Free Press* - 11
Devon (England) - 23
Devonian Period - 23, 25
Dewhirst, Judge - 140
Digger's Den (restaurant) - 53
Door County (Wisconsin) - 33, 44
Drummond Island - 85
Duffy's (restaurant) - 62
Dunkin L. Clinch Yacht Harbor - 45

E

East Bay - 45
East Jordan - 63, 65
Elk Rapids - 48, 50, 53
Emmet County - 85, 86
English Channel - 15

F

Falling Waters Lodge - 37
Farnsworth Point - 118
Fitzgerald, Patti - 143
Fitzgerald, Rockne - 5, 143
Five Wives Press - 79
Font Lake - 83
Forman, Chuck - 143

Fort Mackinac - 12, 13, 111, 113, 129
Fort Mackinaw - 18, 112
Fort Crawford - 142
Fort Howard - 142
Fort Niagara - 142
Fox River - 16
France - 15

G

Galley, The (restaurant) - 108, 129
Garden Bay - 98
Garden Island - 91, 93, 94, 95, 98, 128
Garden Peninsula - 115, 118
Georgian Bay - 21, 115, 125, 130
Gibraltar, Straits of - 15
Government Bay - 124
Government Island - 124
Graham Shoals - 101
Grand Haven - 19
Grand Hotel - 20, 105, 107, 129, 130
Grand Rapids *Times* - 71
Grand Traverse Bay - 11, 33, 43, 44, 48, 49, 53, 55, 85, 129
Grand Traverse Resort - 48
Grays Reef - 101, 115
Grays Reef Passage - 128
Great Britain - 15
Great Lakes Cruising Club - 5, 12
Green Bay - 16, 19, 21, 33, 43, 118, 119, 142
Greensky Hill Church - 62
Greensky, Rev. Peter - 62
Gregg, Phil - 139, 140
Greilickville - 11, 45
Grey Gables (restaurant) - 62

H

Harbor Pier (restaurant) - 74
Harbor Point - 71, 74
Harbor Springs - 71, 73, 74, 75, 129
Harbor Springs Yacht Club - 75
Harbor West (Traverse City) - 45, 47
Hart, Grant - 139, 140
Havighurst, Walter - 18
Hemingway, Ernest - 62
Hessel - 121, 124, 124
Hessel Bay - 124
Hexagonaria Coral - 27
Hiawatha Sportsmen's Club - 118
High Island - 91, 95, 96, 98, 128, 138, 139, 140
Horn's Gaslight Bar - 105
Horse Point - 63
House of David - 98, 138, 139, 140

I

Ice Age - 25
Illinois River Canal - 19
Indian River - 75
Indiana - 59
Interlochen Music School - 62
Irish Boat Shop & Marina - 59, 74
"Israelites" - 138, 139, 140

J

Jolliett, Louis - 16, 91
Jordan Inn - 63
Jordan River - 63, 83
Juillerets (restaurant)- 74

K

Ken's Anchorage - 63
Kings Highway - 83

L

Lake Charlevoix - 58, 59, 62, 63, 128
Lake Genesareth - 83
Lake Huron - 10, 21, 25, 27, 75, 115, 130
Lake Leelanau - 36
Lake Michigan - 9, 10, 11, 16, 19, 21, 25, 27, 28, 29, 33, 36, 37, 43, 44, 45, 49, 53, 55, 59, 66, 71, 75, 80, 86, 91, 115, 118, 127, 128
Lake Superior - 10, 21, 115, 125
Landing, The - 63
Leelanau Peninsula - 29, 33, 36, 49
Lee Point - 48
Leland - 11, 34, 35, 36, 37, 40, 41, 53, 127, 130
Leland Lodge - 37
Les Cheneaux Islands - 121, 124, 125, 129
Lighthouse Point - 49
Little Bob's (restaurant) - 105
Little Mexico (restaurant) - 105
Little Traverse Bay - 11, 55, 69, 70, 71, 129
Louisville (steamer) - 87
Lower Peninsula (Michigan) - 23, 25, 71, 75
Ludington - 16

M

Mackinac, Straits of - 11, 15, 16, 19, 20, 21, 28, 33, 40, 91, 101, 105, 115, 118, 125
Mackinac Bridge - 75, 112
Mackinac County - 16
Mackinac Island - 9, 11, 12, 16, 19, 20, 21, 84, 85, 87, 101,

102, 104, 105, 108, 115, 121, 124, 128, 141, 142
Mackinac Yacht Club - 104
Mackinaw City - 16, 18, 103, 105
Mackinaw County - 85
Majors Shoal - 101
Manistique - 11, 116, 118, 119
Manistique River - 119
Manitou Channel - 127
Manitou Islands - 11, 29
Marquette, Father Jacques - 16, 91
Marquette Bay - 124
Marquette Island - 121
Martin Reef - 124
McCoy, Robert T. - 5, 143
McCulloch, Dr. Hezekiah - 86, 87
Michigan - 9, 10, 20, 23, 25, 27 33, 36, 44, 59, 75, 82, 88, 118, 124
Michigan (battleship) - 87
Michigan Department of Natural Resources - 59
Michigan Travel Bureau - 5, 12, 143
Michigan Waterways Commission - 5, 10, 12, 53, 143
Michilimackinac - 15, 16
Millecoquin's Point - 118
Miracle Mile - 45
Mission House - 20
Mission Point Peninsula - 43, 48, 124
Mississippi River - 16, 19, 82
Montreal - 16, 18
More's Market - 49
Mormons - 81, 82, 83, 84, 85, 86, 87, 88, 94
Moroni - 80
Mount Pisgah - 83
Mullet Lake - 75, 76
Murray Hotel - 105

Muscallonge Bay - 124

N

Naubinway - 117, 118
Nauvoo, Illinois - 81
New Mission Bay - 49
New Mission Point - 40
New York (state) - 80, 82
New York, The (restaurant) - 74
Nicklaus, Jack - 45
Nicolet, Jean - 16, 91
North Channel - 21, 115, 125, 130
North Manitou Island - 28, 40, 41
North Point - 55
Northport - 49, 52, 53, 129
Northport Bay - 49
Northport Point - 49, 53
Northwest Company - 19
Northwest Passage - 16
Northwest Territories - 15

O

Ojibway Indians (Chippewa) - 15, 17, 43
Oklahoma - 25
Old Mission - 44, 53
Old Mission Bay - 48
Oleson's Market - 62
Omena Bay - 49, 53
Omena Yacht Club - 49
Ottawa Indians - 36, 43, 69

P

Panama Canal - 15
Paradise Bay - 84

Paradise Harbor - 94
Park Hotel - 45
Pellston - 105
Penny Island - 124
Pe-te-se-gah - 69
Petoskey - 9, 20, 25, 55, 69, 70, 71, 72, 75, 129
Petoskey, Ignace - 69
Petoskey stone - 25, 27, 31, 59
Pine River - 55, 58, 59, 60, 62, 84, 85, 86
Pine River, Battle of - 85
Pink Panther (restaurant) - 105
Point Betsie - 28
Pomeroy Reef - 124
Pontiac (Indian chief) - 18
Porter, Andrew - 69
Port Inland - 118
Prairie du Chien, Wisconsin - 142
Price, Antje - 135
Protar, Feodor - 88, 95, 135, 136, 137
Purnell, Benjamin (King Ben) - 98, 138, 139, 140
Purnell, Mary (Queen Mary) - 140

Q-R
Rajah Manchore - 82
Revolutionary War - 18
Riccardo's (restaurant) - 62
Ridge Racquet Club - 63
Rock Island, Illinois - 136
Round Island - 101
Round Lake - 58, 59, 128

S
Saginaw Bay - 21
St. Ignace - 16, 18, 105, 108, 109, 129

St. James - 83, 87, 88, 92, 94, 95, 98, 99, 128
St. Martin, Alexis - 141, 142
St. Mary's River - 21, 125
Sault Ste. Marie - 125
Scammons Harbor - 124
Shamrock Bar - 128
Shepler Marine Service - 108
Silurian Sea - 23, 25
Sleeping Bear Dunes National Lakeshore Park - 28, 29, 40
Smith, Joseph - 80, 81, 82
South Manitou Island - 28, 38, 40, 41, 127
South Point - 58
Spain - 15
Stony Point - 94
Straits of Gibraltar - 15
Straits of Mackinac - 11, 15, 16, 19, 20, 21, 28, 33, 40, 91, 101, 105, 115, 118, 125
Strang, James Jesse (King) - 79, 80, 81, 82, 83, 84, 85, 86, 87, 88, 94, 95
Sucker Point - 94
Suez Canal - 15
Suttons Bay - 48, 49, 51, 53
Suttons Point - 48
Suttons Point Shoal - 49

T

Terrace Inn - 71
Traverse City - 9, 11, 20, 44, 45, 46, 47, 48, 53, 129
Ty's (restaurant) - 105

U

U.S. Coast Guard - 11, 62
U.S. Congress - 19, 20

U.S. Corps of Engineers - 76
U.S. Fish and Wildlife Service - 62
Upper Peninsula (Michigan) - 10, 16, 115
Utah - 82

V

Valley of the Giants - 40, 128
Voree, Wisconsin - 81, 82, 87
Vorito - 82

W

Wagon Wheel (restaurant) 63
Walstrom Marina - 74
War of 1812 - 19
Ward, Keith - 2, 143
Water's Edge (restaurant) - 74
Waterfront Inn - 45
Weeks, Robert P. - 79
West Bay - 44
Whiskey Point - 83, 84
Wiggins Point Shoal - 119
Wisconsin - 29, 33, 81, 82
Wright, Billy - 140

X-Y-Z

Yellowstone National Park - 20
Young, Brigham - 81, 82

John B. Torinus

ABOUT THE AUTHOR

John B. Torinus was a journalist for over 50 years, retiring from that profession in 1983. He began his newspaper career with the Green Bay *Press-Gazette* after graduating from Dartmouth College in 1934 and rose through the editorial ranks to the position of executive editor. He took time off to serve as a reserve Army officer in World War II, retiring with the rank of lieutenant colonel. He became editor of the Appleton *Post-Crescent* in 1962.

Torinus began sailing when his teenage daughters took sailing lessons at camp and talked him into buying a Flying Scot. From that 19-foot day sailer, he graduated to a Yankee 24, then a Yankee 28, and finally the 33-foot Ranger he now owns.

His zest for life caused Torinus to take up writing books, beginning in 1982 with the highly successful *The Packer Legend: An Inside Look*, a definitive history of the Green Bay Packers football team and corporation. He updated that title in 1983, and it was released in paperback as *The Packer Legend: Revised Edition*. It has been updated again and released in hardcover again for the fall of 1985.

One success deserves another, so Torinus wrote *Summer Sail: Cruising Green Bay's Historic Waters* (also known as *Summer Sail I*) in 1984. This critically acclaimed work went into its second printing in 1985.

Torinus and his wife Louise live in De Pere, Wisconsin but have maintained a summer home at Egg Harbor in Door County, Wisconsin for many years.

If you have enjoyed *Summer Sail II: Visiting Northern Lake Michigan* **and would like to read** *Summer Sail: Cruising Green Bay's Historic Waters*, **you may either order directly from the publisher -** Laranmark Press, Box 253, Neshkoro, WI 54960 - **or you may purchase a copy at any of the fine bookstores listed below.**

In Wisconsin:
Abby's Bookstore, *Beaver Dam*; Alcove Bookshop, *Burlington*; Booklands, *Neenah, Ripon, Antigo, Wausau, Minocqua, Eagle River, Stevens Point, Rhinelander, Shawano*; Book Shop, *Rice Lake*; Book World, *Janesville*; Bookworm, *Boulder Junction*; Books Up The Road, *Washington Island*; Breadloaf Bookshop, *Lake Geneva*; Conkey's Bookstore, *Appleton*; Des Forges, *Milwaukee*; Falls Bookstore, *Menomonee Falls*; Janke's Bookstore, *Wausau*; Knot Hole Bookstore, *Green Bay*; Little Professors, *Appleton, West Bend, Oconomowoc*; M'Ellen's, *Fond du Lac*; Mallach's Bookstore, *Watertown*; Martha Merrell's, *Racine, Waukesha*; Moseley's, *Madison*; Nastall's Books & Things, *Milwaukee, Bayview*; Passtime Books, *Ephraim*; Readmore, *LaCrosse*; 20th Century Books, *Madison*; University Bookstores, *Madison, Hilldale*; Webster's Books, *Milwaukee*; Worley's Bookstore, Sturgeon Bay; Book Nook, *Whitefish Bay*; Dickens Discount Books, *Madison, Kenosha*; Schwartz's Bookstore, *Milwaukee*.

In Michigan:
Abby Road, *Kalamazoo*; Apollo Schultz Bookseller, *Gaylord*; Between The Covers, *Harbor Springs*; Birmingham Bookstore, *Birmingham*; The Book End, *Fenton*; Book Harbor, *Mt. Pleasant*; Book House, *Jonesville*; Bookshelf, *Bay City*; Book Shelf, *Union Lake*; Books Etc., *Hastings*; Book Tree, *Grand Rapids*; Canterbury Bookstore, *Escanaba*; Cadillac Newscenter, *Cadillac*; Community Newscenters, *Ann Arbor, Lansing, East Lansing, Okemos, Holt*; Heritage House, *Dearborn*; Horizon Books, *Traverse City, Petoskey, Beulah*; Jay's Book Mart, *Jackson*; Jocundry's, *East Lansing*; Literary News Center, *Charlevoix*; Little Professor, *Brighton, Traverse City*; Log Mark Bookstore, *Cheboygan*; Metro News Center, *Birmingham*; Reading Express, *Farmington Hills*; Read Mor, *Battle Creek*; Tom Sawyer, *Kalamazoo*; Student Book Exchange, *Mt. Pleasant*; Student Bookstore, *East Lansing*; Sue's Book Shelf, *Marshall*; Thompson News Service, *Traverse City*; Volume I, *Petoskey*; West Main Book Rack, *Kalamazoo*; Young & Welshans, *Flint*; Gerry's Book Co., *Wyoming*.

In Illinois:
Alamo II, *Normal*; Anderson's Paradise Bookstore, *Naperville*; The Book Bin, *Northbrook*; Book Nook, *LaGrange*; Book Rack, *Bolingbrook*; Books And More, *Kankakee*; Browse Around Bookstore, *Crystal Lake*; Chapter One, *Freeport*; Fireside Books, *Crystal Lake*; Lora & Wally Griggs Booksellers, *Woodstock*; Scudder & Hall Books, *Chicago*; Kroch's & Brentano's, *Chicago*.

In Indiana:
Book World, *Mishawaka*.

Also at B. Dalton Booksellers and Waldenbooks throughout the Great Lakes region.